# Krazy Tales From the World of Golf

# Krazy Tales From the World of Golf

*90 Funny, Original, and True Stories*

GAIL K. HOLDEN

**Krazy Tales from the World of Golf: 90 Funny, Original, and True Stories**

# Contents

## _PRELUDE_

When a fun-loving group of ex-hockey players trade their hockey sticks for golf clubs, anything can happen. These are the hilarious tales from the group's thirty plus annual summertime sojourns into Montana and beyond. All stories are true and very original. So, buckle your seat belts and join us on this unbelievable ninety story journey.

# *<u>ACKNOWLEDGMENTS</u>*

To all those brave souls who had the courage to board the Montana Golf Trip bus, knowing that they could be, and probably would be, subjected to abuse and humiliation from their "friends". Without those courageous folks, this book would not have been possible.

# *INTRODUCTION*

I f you enjoy the game of golf, or just appreciate a humorous story, you will enjoy this book. It is a compilation of ninety separate and funny stories and events, all of which are somehow associated with the game of golf.

All the stories in this book are true. The events described herein really happened. The author was either present when these events occurred, and observed them first hand, or was part of a group of ex-hockey players turned golfing buddies, who were directly involved in the events themselves. Not all events happened on a golf course. Some occurred during the "social hours" following golf matches and some even occurred before the golf matches even started. But all are somehow linked to the game of golf.

In order to fully enjoy this book, it is important to know the characters. And it is equally important to know their backgrounds and the "connections" they have to each other.

Spokane, WA has been an exceptional hockey town for the past 50 years. Many championship teams have been based in Spokane including four Allan Cup winning teams and a Memorial Cup winning team.

In 1970 the Spokane Jets became the first American based team to ever win the Allan Cup, which is emblematic of being the top Senior hockey team in Canada and the United States. The Spokane team went on to win a total of four Allan Cups in the 1970s and 1980s. And the Spokane Chiefs won the Memorial Cup in 1991 as the top Junior hockey team in Canada and the United States.

Over the years it has been common for players coming to

Spokane to play hockey, to remain in Spokane after their playing careers ended, and make Spokane their home. Many attended universities in the Spokane area and many others found employment in the city. They married, had families, and became pillars of the community.

The Spokane hockey community is comprised of professionals in every area of business including, accountants, doctors, physical therapists, lawyers, restaurant owners, real estate people, private business owners, contractors, and school teachers, to name just a few. Golf is a favorite pass time for most of them.

A brief description of Spokane's hockey history and Spokane's hockey community is necessary because the stories in this publication involve, with few exceptions, people who are somehow related to Spokane's hockey community.


It was the Spring of 1985. The Spokane Flames Junior hockey team was holding an auction-dinner to raise funds for the next hockey season. One of the former Spokane Jets hockey players bid on and won, the use of the Flames team bus, to be used over a three-day weekend, sometime during that upcoming summer. The bus was a converted Greyhound bus and seated about 40 passengers. The only stipulation on the use of the bus was that the person driving the bus have a Commercial Driver's License (CDL) which was required so that the insurance coverage for the bus would be in force.

The winning bidder really had no plans or ideas for the use of the bus for that three-day weekend---he was merely trying to support the local hockey club when he placed his winning bid.

During the weeks following the auction, discussions were had among the winning bidder and several of his hockey buddies seeking ideas on to how the bus could best be put to use. It was finally decided to get a group of guys together and head to the Kalispel-Whitefish, Montana area, some 250 miles east of Spokane, to play golf for three days. The dates for the trip would be the second weekend in August.

Thus, began what has now become known as the "Montana Golf Trip". The trip has now become an annual affair for thirty plus consecutive years and is always held on the second weekend of August. This is a "hockey guys" trip and usually 24 to 28 golfers go on the trip. Nobody much cares what the quality of the respective golfers are. The guys on the trip are there to have fun.

The trip destination for 80% of the bus trips has been the State of Montana but the group has also traveled to golf courses in Washington State and British Columbia. No matter the destination, the trip is always referred to as the "Montana Golf Trip".

This book is a blow-by-blow description of many of the most hilarious stories and events that have evolved from those golf trips. These stories are true and original. Many of the stories took place after the golf matches had ended for the day and the "social periods" had begun.

As you will see, the guys making these trips have great, and sometimes wild, imaginations, and will do almost anything to embarrass another group member.

The names of all participants in the following stories and events have been assigned an anonymous first name or "nick name".

So come along with us and relive some unbelievable golf related stories that will keep you thoroughly entertained and will hopefully provide you with laughable memories for years to come.

# FIRST MONTANA GOLF TRIP
## --- AUGUST 1985

The first "Montana Golf Trip" took place in August 1985. There were eight guys on board the bus as it left the Spokane city limits headed for Kalispel, Montana, some 250 miles distant. Here is a summary of that first trip, and some of the events that took place on that trip.

## *1. OOPS, SORRY 'BOUT THAT*

t was the first day with the bus. There were eight guys on board including the cocky 20-year-old driver, Lefty, who happened to have the necessary Commercial Driver's License (CDL) to validate the insurance coverage for the use of the bus. Although Lefty had a CDL, he had never driven a bus before, but in his mind that "was no big deal'.

The bus had been on the road less than one hour as it headed eastbound towards the State of Montana. It was about 11:00 am on a Friday. As it approached the small town of Newport, Washington, about 40 miles north of Spokane, Freddy, one of the bus occupants, hollered from the back of the bus "Is there a liquor store in this town?" Lunker, who happened to be one of the eight guys on the bus, was very familiar with the town because he owned and operated a pizza restaurant in Newport. He gave Lefty directions to the town's only liquor store which was located on a steep incline in downtown Newport.

There were no vacant parking places in front of the liquor store so Lefty double parked the bus in front of the store next to a brand-new Buick automobile. The Buick was so new that it still had the temporary paper license plate taped to its rear window.

The boys all got off the bus, went inside the liquor store, made their purchases, and returned to the bus, while Lefty sat in the driver's seat waiting for the boys to return. When all the guys were back on board, and while the bus door was still open, Lefty released the parking brake so he could start moving the bus forward up the incline that the bus was parked on. When Lefty took his foot off the brake, the bus started rolling backwards, and because Lefty forgot to close the door, the door struck the side of the brand-new Buick. Before Lefty could stop the bus, it had rolled backwards about 10 feet with the bus door jammed into the side of the Buick, leaving a huge crease stretching the entire length of the spanking new Buick.

When Lefty finally got the bus stopped, he looked around to see if anyone had witnessed the creasing. No one seemed to be around so Lefty drove up the hill and out of town.

We had been on the road less than 60 minutes and Lefty had already given us reason to doubt his driving abilities. Where in hell did we get this kid?

# 2. MUSICAL CHAIRS---AT 70 MPH

The "auction" bus was chugging along nicely at 70 mph. Lefty, the trusted CDL driver with no prior bus driving experience, was seated behind the wheel. We were 40 miles east of Newport, approaching the Montana State line.

The remaining seven occupants were at the back of the bus drinking beer and playing that great Canadian card game called "Stook". Stook is one of the greatest card games ever invented. It is much like Blackjack but with a few twists---the main one being that the dealer wins if he and the player he is playing against have a numerical tie. All players want to deal because of this "tie" rule and the substantial odds that are associated with ties. Fortunes have been won and lost in a matter of seconds playing Stook.

As the bus rolled along towards the Montana line, it seemed that Lefty was hitting every chuckhole and bump on the roadway, thus causing the cards and betting money laying on the card table to be thrown into the air or onto the floor of the bus, making it almost impossible to carry on a civilized game of Stook. After many unheeded complaints being yelled at Lefty to "slow down" and "get the bus out of the ditch", Nellie finally said "I am going to go up and drive this son of a bitch". Nellie then walked up to the front of the bus and told Lefty to pull over so he (Nellie) could drive. Lefty, being tired of all the insults flowing from the back of the bus, immediately got out of the driver's seat while the bus was still traveling down the highway, and said "here, it's all yours". Lefty immediately vacated the driver's seat and started for the back of the bus. The driver's seat was vacant for a couple of seconds until Nellie realized that the bus needed a driver, and jumped into the driver's seat.

Lefty joined the Stook game and Nellie became a bus driver for the first time in his life. The bus went from being "insured" to being "uninsured" within two seconds and no one on board seemed too concerned.

# 3. "I'LL TWIST YOU FOR A BEER"

The bus pulled into a bar on the outskirts of Libby, Montana. It seemed like a good place to take a break and have a beer or two. Plus, the new bus driver, Nellie, needed a break. After all, although this was his first "bus driving job", he knew that the law required him to take rest breaks every once in a while, in the interests of safety.

As the group of eight made their way into the bar, they couldn't help but notice several motorcycles in the parking lot. Upon entering the establishment, the group saw about twenty heavily tattooed guys in black leather jackets, bandanas, and motorcycle boots. This would be a perfect group to play a little pool with, join for a beer or two, and just get to know a little better. Plus, if things ever got out of hand, there were only twenty of them.

It was a small, cozy bar, the kind that was perfect for rubbing shoulders and making new friends. And with about a dozen beers under the belts of the Spokane eight, introductions would be a whole lot easier.

Mac immediately approached the only pool table in the bar, where two "leathers" were in the middle of a game. "My buddy, Griz and I will play you a game of pool. Losers buy the winners a beer. You in?" challenged Mac.

"Yeah, we're in. By the way my name's Clyde and this here is Pooper. Bet you can't guess how he got the name," laughed Clyde. Mac ignored the question even though he thought he had the probable answer.

Within just a few minutes the "leathers" had each earned themselves a beer. They were beginning to like these foreigners.

Because the bar was so small, everyone inside was pretty much shoulder to shoulder. The eight bar stools were occupied as were the 15 or so chairs that surrounded the three or four tables.

The two groups actually got along quite well for the first hour or so. Several beers were consumed, some more pool was played, and some good country tunes blared from the juke box.

One of the "leathers" was a big, muscular guy who had his sleeves cut off at the shoulders with tattoos lining his arms. Obviously, he had pumped some weights in his day. This was not a guy to mess with. But fortunately, he seemed to be a good-natured guy. But all that was about to change when Knob decided to challenge him to an arm-wrestling contest. "I'll twist you for two pitchers of beer" challenged Knob. The sleeveless "leather" looked at the scrawny, 5-foot 9-inch, 160-pound challenger, and couldn't believe what he was hearing. He asked: "Did I hear you right?" "You sure did" replied Knob.

The two combatants walked over to the closest table, kicked two guys out of their chairs, and sat down facing each other across the table. All the guys crowded around as the contestants snarled at each other.

The two men placed their arms out on the table, grabbed each other's hand, and one of the guys said: "GO." The big "leather" held Knob's arm in place for a few seconds, just toying with him, and then "bang", he slammed the back of the challenger's hand into the table top with so much force that he almost split the table in two. He then said to Knob: "Two pitchers of Kokanee please." Knob looked up at the huge man and without any fear said: "I said I would twist you for two pitchers of beer. I did that. I didn't say I would win. Get my boys two pitchers of Bud please."

This is where things got interesting. These little "word games" didn't have any place in the lives of the bikers. The big "leather" grabbed the table where the two were seated, flipped it over like it was a flapjack, and grabbed Knob by the neck. The big "leather's" eyes were now the size of saucers and the veins in his neck were standing on end as he said to Knob: "That will be two pitchers of Kokanee please and I want them now".

A couple of the other guys from the Spokane eight jumped in and said: "The beers are on the way. He was just having fun." The big guy let go of Knob's neck, the beers were delivered to the bikers, and things quieted down.

Not long after, the Spokane eight decided it was time to depart the Libby bar, knowing to a man that they had indeed dodged a bullet.

# 4. WELCOME TO THE OUTLAW INN, KALISPEL, MONTANA

After stopping at every watering hole between Spokane and Kalispel, MT, it was time to get to bed. It was 2:00 AM. It had been a long day. Beers and drinks had been consumed. Many Stook games had been played. Reservations for eight were waiting at the Outlaw Inn and the guys had a tee time for 9:00 o'clock the next morning.

At the last bar stop in Kalispel, a head count was taken---there was only seven guys on board---one had disappeared---it was Freddy. No one seemed to know where he was---but he had last been seen in the company of a tall, long-legged cowgirl.

The seven remaining guys decided to head to the Outlaw Inn without Freddy, and check in. They knew that somehow Freddy would find his way back to the hotel before the bus had to leave for the golf course the next morning. He always showed up.

However, there was one little problem---Lefty, the CDL driver, was no longer able to talk let alone drive. The cocky 20-year-old had over imbibed on that great Montana whiskey.

The only other guy with bus driving "experience" was Nellie and when asked whether he was okay to drive, he replied "Hell yo I am five". With that solid assurance, Nellie again took the controls of the bus and the group headed through the City of Kalispel to the Outlaw Inn.

The Outlaw Inn is a very nice hotel. There is a nice drive-up area, located under a permanent canopy, just a few feet outside the registration desk. This makes it very handy for guests to get out of their vehicles and enter the hotel to register. It also protects the guests from the weather.

When Nellie maneuvered the bus into this drive-up area, it was about 2:15AM. There was another vehicle parked close to the guest registration area, and right next to the side of the hotel. We later learned that this vehicle belonged to the night desk manager and rather than parking his vehicle in the main guest parking lot that was located about 40 paces away from the hotel door, the manager decided to park immediately next to the hotel in close proximity to where guests would temporarily park their vehicles when registering. It was a matter of convenience for the manager---it saved him 40 paces of walking---but it could also interfere with the vehicles of approaching guests---especially if the guests were approaching in a Greyhound bus and the driver was a rookie.

As Nellie pulled the Greyhound into the area under the hotel canopy, he misjudged the distance between the passenger side of the bus and the manager's vehicle. All of a sudden there was a loud crunching sound---much like the sound created when two vehicles collide. Everyone on board the bus was now wide awake, except for Lefty, the kid. We were able to observe the manager's car being mangled between the bus and the side of the hotel.

Nellie, ever the genius, realized that he had a problem on his hands. He stopped the bus, backed up, and then proceeded to pull the bus around to the main guest parking area. The boys unloaded their suitcases, went to the hotel registration desk, got their room keys and retired for the evening. The desk manager did not learn until the end of his shift several hours later, that his vehicle had been damaged. By then he did not know how his vehicle had been damaged or who was responsible. There was no obvious damage done to the Greyhound.

The following Monday morning Knob, an attorney, was at work in his Spokane office when the phone rang. It was the President of the Spokane Flames Hockey Club—the owner of the bus. The President said he had just received a call from the Outlaw Inn claiming that the bus was in some kind of accident with a car owned by the Hotel's night manager, and that the car had suffered extensive damages. Knob told the President not to worry, that there was really no problem, and if there were any further calls from the Outlaw Inn, to refer those calls to Knob's office.

An hour later Knob got a call from the Outlaw Inn. The conversation went something like this:

Outlaw: "I am calling about a collision that occurred over the weekend at the Outlaw Inn. It seems that your bus collided with our night manager's car causing extensive damages to the car."

Knob: "I am so glad you called. In fact, I was just getting ready to call you. I represent the Hockey Club and the bus driver".

"The passengers on board that bus had called the Outlaw Inn many hours in advance of their 2:00 am arrival time to report that they would be driving through the night and would be arriving late. They arrived at the front of your hotel at approximately 2:00 am. Upon pulling the bus up under the Canopy area, an area reserved for guests checking into your hotel, the bus driver found what apparently was your night manager's car, illegally parked within that area reserved for paying guests.

Yes, there was a collision between the bus and your night manager's vehicle; however, the collision would never have happened if your night manager had parked his vehicle in the main guest area where his vehicle should have been parked that night. Your night manager was too lazy to walk the 40 paces from the main parking area to the front door of the hotel.

What I need from you, and the reason I was going to call you today, is the name, address, and phone number of your liability insurance company because it now appears that the bus may have suffered significant damage from that collision and a claim may be made against your hotel. Do you have that information for me?"

Several seconds of silence.

Knob: "Excuse me sir, but do you have that information for me?"

Outlaw: "Not at this time."

Knob: "Can you get me that information?"

Outlaw: "I will see what I can do."

Knob: "One other thing: For your information, my client, the bus driver, has never before been in an accident of any kind, during his entire driving career. He is devastated that his record has been tarnished because of the laziness of your front desk clerk. This was no way for your Hotel to treat late arriving guests who had shown confidence in your Hotel by selecting it over the many other hotels in the area. I look forward to receiving the requested insurance information."

End of call.


No one ever again heard from the Outlaw Inn concerning the accident.

No "hidden" damages were ever found on the bus.

The Hockey Club never learned the full extent of the "accident".

The relationship between the Hockey Club and the golfing group remains strong to this day.

Leftie, the cocky kid with the CDL, eventually learned how to drive.

Nellie never again drove a bus.


Other than the above, the first "Montana Golf Trip" was uneventful. However, there would be plenty of other "action" during the future golf trips into Montana and other locations. Below are some of the most memorable stories.

# THIRTY MORE YEARS OF FUNNY STORIES

## *5. MOOOOO!!*

It was a nice, warm August day. The bus had just dropped off 24 golfers at St. Eugene's Mission Golf Course located a few minutes outside of Cranbrook, British Columbia, Canada. This was the second day of a three-day golfing excursion into British Columbia. The golfers separated into their designated foursomes and started play.

There is a beautiful little par three on the front nine of St. Eugene's. The tee shot is from a steeply elevated tee to a large green below. The distance is about 150 yards.

There is a spectacular view from the tee box. Off to the left and down below, is the Kootenay River, which meanders throughout the golf course. On the other side of the river is some beautiful and lush green pasture land where cows wander aimlessly while grazing in the field. Those grazing cows were about 150 yards from the tee box.

As one group made its way to this par three tee box area, it was observed that another foursome was on the green, ready to putt out. A third group was waiting for the green to clear before hitting their tee shots.

Tim just happened to be in the foursome that was waiting for the green to clear. Having a little time on his hands, Tim pulled an iron from his bag and said: "I've got $5.00 that says I can hit one of those cows grazing in the field across the river". Someone quickly spoke up and said: "You're on". Tim threw his ball on the ground and lined up his shot. He hit a hooded three iron across the river and the ball struck one of those cows in the side of the neck. The cow let out a loud bellow and began running down the pasture.

The "MOOOOOOO" was heard around the golf course. Tim collected his $5.00 bet.

# 6. WHEN OPPORTUNITY KNOCKS ...

We were on our way to the Lochsaw River in Idaho to "run the rapids". There were 12 of us in the motor home. It was a Friday in July. We were due to check in at the white-water rafting camp later that evening. We were to spend two days rafting the Lochsaw River with professional guides.

But first, we would stop and play a round of golf at the Lewiston, Idaho, Golf and Country Club, located about 100 miles from Spokane, WA, our home base.

Things were moving smoothly on the golf course. There was some beer drinking going on as well as the usual betting games. Nothing too exciting and nothing out of the ordinary.

Freddy's four some was playing the 17 th hole. One of his playing partners was Lunker, and he and Freddy were riding together in a cart.

Lunker is not against screwing with a guy's equipment now and then, if the opportunity presents itself. On this particular day, the opportunity presented itself.

Lunker found a dead crow laying in the fairway. As Freddy was taking a fairway shot, Lunker picked up the dead crow and placed it inside one of the zippered pockets on Freddy's golf bag. Lunker zipped the pocket shut and the four some completed its round of golf. Freddy put his golf bag back in the motor home not realizing he had a new "passenger".

Freddy did not play his next golf match until about one month later. It was a rainy day and Freddy went looking for his rain gear. He unzipped the pocket where he kept his rain gear and was almost kayoed by a terrible smell. When he looked inside, he found the dead crow, now covered with maggots, laying on top of his rain gear.

Freddy's rain gear and bag were ruined as was his golf outing.

# 7. JUST A "SHITTY" ROUND OF GOLF

I t was a hot Friday afternoon in August. All the guys had put in a long, tough weak working their various jobs in and around the Spokane area. The boys had worked up a pretty good thirst and, as was customary, they decided to stop in at Geno's Red Lion BBQ Restaurant and Pub for a cold one. The restaurant is located in downtown Spokane. Geno is a former Spokane Jets/Flyers hockey player having played for ten seasons.

On this particular day, Nellie, Nacs, and Knob, all arrived at the Pub at about 4:30 PM and took a table in the bar area. Geno, the owner of the establishment and a guy who would rather talk than work, soon joined his three friends at the table. After a couple of hours of sipping on beers and discussing world events, Nacs suggested that maybe the group should play a round of golf the next morning.

Before we go any further with this story, it is important to know that Nacs was an 11 handicap, Nellie and Geno were both 15 handicaps, and Knob carried a 28 handicap.

When Nacs suggested the round of golf, Nellie immediately asked "Who gets the little shit"?---meaning who will be the unlucky guy who is forced to take the Knob for a partner. Geno immediately said "I'll take him" and the match was on. Everybody agreed that Geno and Knob would get a stroke a hole, with no strokes given on the par threes. It was further agreed to play at the Deer Park Course located about 20 miles north of Spokane. The stakes were $1.00 per hole per partner. The trailing team could go "double or nothing" at any time during the match.

As the evening wore on, Knob, feeling a little bit "hurt" because neither Nacs nor Nellie wanted him for a partner, pulled Geno aside and said: "I am going to buy some Ex-lax and put it in Nacs' coffee cup tomorrow morning before golf". Geno replied "We can do better

23

than that. I just happen to have a colonoscopy scheduled for Monday morning. I just picked up the powder and juice that I am supposed to mix together and drink the night before my procedure. It cleans out the insides in a real hurry. I will get you some of that powder and you can work your magic."

Wow---what a stroke of luck!

Just before heading home for the evening, Geno gave Knob the magic vial that he had in his office at the bar.

It was about 8:30 on Saturday morning. It was a most beautiful day. The birds were chirping and the sun was shining. A perfect day for golf.

The foursome had agreed to meet at the Yak Bar and Restaurant, on the North side of Spokane, for coffee before heading out to the Deer Park Golf Course. Knob arrived a few minutes earlier than the rest. He gave the waitress a $5.00 bill to keep a secret. Knob then poured the powder from the vial into a clean coffee cup and instructed the waitress to pour coffee into the cup after Nacs ordered his coffee. Nacs, Nellie, and Geno all arrived shortly thereafter, and true to habit, Nacs ordered a coffee. The waitress poured the coffee as instructed and delivered it to Nacs who drank the coffee in short order.

About a half hour later, the four men piled into Knob's car and headed north towards the Golf Course.

They hadn't gone six blocks when Nacs said: "Knob, would you mind pulling into my office on the way out of town. I need to pick something up".

"Not a problem Nacs".

Knob pulled into the parking area at Nacs office building. Nacs went inside and returned five minutes later. Nacs was not carrying anything when he returned to the car nor did he say anything more about his need to stop at his office.

The guys continued on to the Deer Park Course. Knob parked

in front of the Pro Shop so all could unload their clubs. That is, all except for Nacs. As soon as the car stopped in front of the Pro Shop, Nacs asked Nellie to grab his clubs---Nacs headed to the Mens Room. When he returned from the bathroom, Nellie asked "What's the matter?" Nacs replied that he had a little bit of an upset stomach but "it should be fine now".

The boys immediately headed for the first tee box. Geno and Knob shared a cart as did their opponents, Nellie and Nacs.

It is important to know that Nacs is a "whale" of a man standing about 6 feet one inch tall and tipping the elevator scales at close to 300 pounds. Under normal circumstances, he has a long stride, but not this day.

Nacs is an 11 handicap and consistently drives the ball about 260 yards.

When the foursome arrived at the first tee box, all got out of the carts and grabbed their drivers. As they made their way to the tee off location, it was obvious that Nacs' stride was much shorter than usual---he seemed to be taking very short, careful steps, much like when a person is walking over an icy driveway.

As he bent over to tee up his ball, Nacs seemed a little hesitant and was not the usual jovial, cocky guy his paying partners were accustomed to seeing. He addressed his ball in a rather unusual fashion---usually his legs are shoulder width apart---but on this day his legs were very close together and his knees were almost touching. With his first swing of the day, he did not rotate the hips at all, but swung only with his arms. He hit the ball about 80 yards. His partner, Nellie, said: "what the hell was that"?

The rest of hole No. 1 was more of the same. Nacs hit each shot using his arms only and got very little distance from any of his shots. He registered an eight on the easy par 4 hole which was playing about 340 yards. Nacs and Nellie were each down $1.00 heading into the second hole.

Before teeing off on the second hole, Nellie gave Nacs a little pep talk and reminded him that they had a money match going on and he, Nellie would just as soon not lose to "those two assholes we are playing against". Nacs nodded his head in agreement.

The second hole is a 475-yard par five. When it was Nacs turn to tee off, he had the same approach as he did on the first hole---arms only and no involvement of the hips or legs. His drive went 90 yards. He took another eight on the second hole causing his partner to use several profane words about his golfing ability.

Nacs and Nellie were now down $2.00 each.

As the crew made its way to hole number three, Nacs spotted a Porta Potty at the tee box of hole No. four and headed straight arrow to the shitter. By the time Nacs returned to the third tee box, the other three guys had already teed off. Nellie said to Nacs: "I doubled up here so it's about time you pulled your head out of your ass". However, Nacs didn't feel "secure" in teeing off in normal fashion and once again hit a very poor drive, followed by six additional poor-quality shots, ending with a seven on another easy par four hole.

Nacs and Nellie were now down $4.00 each.

Holes 4, 5, and 6, were much like the first three holes---Nacs played poorly and he and Nellie lost all three holes after doubling up on each of those holes. They were now down $32.00 each, even though Nacs took another potty break before teeing off on hole No.6.

After losing six holes in a row, Nellie was getting pretty frustrated with his usually reliable partner. He pulled him aside before teeing off on seven and said: "What the hell is wrong with you today?" Nacs replied: "I just have an unsettled stomach and I feel like I have a touch of diarrhea. I just took another dump so I think I should be okay now." Nellie said: "Okay let's go after them".

They doubled the bet again on hole No. 7---but the results were the same. Nacs couldn't play worth a shit---no pun intended. They were now down $64.00 each with two holes to play on the front nine.

Nellie refused to bet on holes 8 and 9 hoping that somehow Nacs would get "his shit together" for the back nine.

Wouldn't you know it, Nacs headed into the clubhouse shitter at the turn. He also bought himself a hot dog and coke and declared confidently to his partner: "I am now ready to go".

On to hole No. 10. At the tee box, Nellie, believing that his partner had now corrected whatever ailed him, said to his opponents: "Okay assholes, we're doubling you here".

Hole No. 10 is a straight away hole of about 400 yards with water on the left side. Any drive to the right side is safe. Geno and Knob hit safe, but not long, drives up the right side. Nellie followed with a 260-yard drive right down the middle.

The ever-dapper Nacs then stepped up to the tee box. He was wearing a nice pair of tan slacks with a red golf shirt. He appeared confident on the tee box. He addressed his ball with his legs shoulder width apart, just like the Nacs of old.

For the first time that day, Nacs made a full swing at the ball, using his legs and rotating his hips. And then it happened---a loud eruption bellowed from the rear of his massive body. His once tan slacks quickly became two tone. And try as he did, Nacs was not able to stem the blast.

To add to his predicament, Nac's drive went straight left into the pond.

Nellie was furious---if they lost this hole, they would each owe $128.00. He screamed at Nacs calling him every name he could think of. Nacs said: "I am sorry Nellie. I thought I was okay, but obviously I still have some intestinal problems. Maybe I should just shut it down for the day".

Nellie said: "If you quit now, I am out $128.00." They decided to play on.

Geno and Knob were laughing so hard they were crying.

Nacs and Nellie lost hole No. 10 and were now down $128.00 each.

There was no more betting on holes 11, 12, 13, and 14. Nellie refused to ride with Nacs on those holes electing instead to walk. Nacs hit the shitter again on holes 11 and 13.

At the 15th tee box, Nacs told Nellie that he was feeling a little better and suggested that they might want to double up again. Nellie refused. They lost hole No. 15 but no bet had been made.

Halfway through hole No. 16, Nacs made another detour to the shitter. But they still lost the hole.

As they were waiting to tee off on No. 17, Nacs said he thought his system was fully cleaned out and he thought they should double up again because they were down $128.00 each with only two holes to go. Nellie asked: "Are you sure you can swing the club". Nacs said: "Yes, I am sure".

They doubled up again on hole 17. Nacs actually played much better than he had all day, but they still lost the hole. They were now down $256.00 each with one hole to play. They had lost all 17 holes. Nellie was pissed—but there was a glimmer of hope in the way Nacs had played hole 17.

As they reached the 18th tee box, Nellie asked Geno and Knob: "Among friends, would you guys be willing to give us a stroke on the last hole if we double up? You are into us pretty good right now". The response was: "Certainly".

The 18th hole was uneventful. Nacs played pretty well. He did not seem to be bothered by the "stomach ailment" that had bothered him much of the day. Undoubtedly, his numerous trips to the various bathrooms over the previous four or five hours, had pretty much cleaned him out to the point where he was finally able to swing normally without being in fear of soiling his pants.

Despite the improvement in Nac's game on the last hole, and despite getting a stroke, Nacs and Nellie lost again. They were each down $512.00 with no holes to play.

Nacs hit the mens room for "a final clean up" before heading back to Spokane.

On the twenty-minute return trip from Deer Park to Spokane, Nacs and Nellie sat in the back seat. Not a word was spoken. Nellie was fuming. Geno and Knob kept their front windows open all the way to Spokane.

As the group entered the Spokane city limits, Geno suggested they go to Mama Mia's restaurant to have a beer, a bite to eat, and "square up". All agreed.

The guys spent the next couple of hours at Mama Mia's. Not much was mentioned about the golf game. As the night wore on, everyone relaxed a little and enjoyed the dinner.

When the guys got ready to leave the restaurant and head to their respective homes, Nacs suggested that he and Nellie "pick up the bill"---it was obvious that this generous gesture was an attempt to get Geno and Knob to respond by saying "let's call it square". That is exactly what happened and everyone shook hands and agreed that the bet had been fully paid.

When all four guys had made their way outside the restaurant, Knob turned to Geno and asked: "Geno, what time is your colonoscopy on Monday"?

It took a minute to register, but Nellie eventually looked at Nacs and the two of them finally realized why Nacs had experienced the unusual "stomach ailment" that day. Many obscene names were directed towards the winners of that day's golf match and many promises were made insinuating that paybacks would be in order.

Nacs felt fine the next day but he never wore his tan slacks again.

Nellie forgave Nacs for his poor golf outing and partnered up with him in later golf matches.

Geno's Monday colonoscopy went without a hitch, although his doctor chuckled when he heard the story.

Knob just smiled and thanked Nacs and Nellie for a most memorable day.

# 8. WELCOME TO THE GAME OF GOLF

He had only played a dozen rounds in his life. But Tuna loved the outdoors and loved being with his friends. Plus, he didn't mind sipping on a cold beer now and then. Such was the case on a hot summer day in Spokane, WA when Tuna teed it up with a few of his buddies at Downriver Golf Course.

Tuna got carted up with his friend, Nacs, on that day and away they went. Tuna was the driver.

It is important to note that Tuna is a large man, standing 6 feet 4 inches and weighing in at 250 pounds. He played three years of college football on scholarship at Eastern State University. After his football days ended, he became a top-notch food salesman in the Spokane area.

Nacs is a very experienced golfer and carries an 11 handicap. Tuna rarely breaks 100 even on a good day. He is very inexperienced when it comes to golf rules, golf etiquette, and the like. Tuna had never before played at Downriver Golf Course.

The round was quite uneventful until the fourth hole when Tuna's golf bag fell off the cart as he and Nacs made their way down the fairway. Tuna circled back, picked up the clubs, strapped them back on and said: "I am sure I strapped the bag on". Nacs said: "I have played out here a lot, and some of the straps on these carts don't hold very well".

They continued on their round. While driving up the hill towards the 6th tee box, Tuna's bag fell off a second time, this time scattering several of his clubs on the hillside. Again, he circled back, picked up his clubs and bag, and re-strapped the bag to the cart. He again commented that he thought he had properly secured his bag to the cart and again Nacs told him that he likely had a faulty strap.

When the bag and clubs fell off a third time while going up the 9th fairway, Tuna was pissed. Nacs again suggested that the cart had a bad strap and advised Tuna to report the problem to the Pro Shop at the turn and request another cart. The cart number was 27 and Nacs told Tuna to tell the Pro Shop that it was cart 27 that was causing the problem.

When they drove up to the Pro Shop at the turn, they ran into Elmer, Nac's friend, and the guy who makes and repairs golf clubs at Downriver. Nacs gave Elmer a wink. Tuna then relayed the problems he had been having with the cart strap. Elmer looked at the cart and said: "You are driving that Number 27 cart. We have had nothing but trouble with that darn strap on that cart. Why don't you guys transfer your clubs to another cart." Tuna and Nacs then transferred their clubs to another cart and headed for the back nine.

As Tuna and Nacs made their way towards the 11th hole, Tuna's bag fell off again. This time he was madder than hell and said: "I am going to jam this cart right up that Pro's ass when I get back to the Pro Shop".

Nacs was able to calm Tuna down and they continued on their way.

Everything was fine until they started up the hill towards the 18th green when Tuna's bag again fell off, scattering his clubs all over the hill side. Tuna was really pissed this time and was steaming as he putted out on the last green. Nacs, always the steadying influence, suggested nicely that Tuna report the problem to the Head Pro.

After removing his clubs from the cart and placing them in his car, Tuna marched into the Pro Shop demanding a face-to-face meeting with the Head Pro and demanding that he get a refund for the cost of the cart. The Assistant paged the Head Pro, who was also a good friend of Nacs, and the Head Pro appeared shortly thereafter. Tuna started yelling at the Head Pro telling him that the straps on the carts were horseshit and demanding a refund on the cart rental. Nacs just stood by smiling as Tuna let loose on the Head Pro.

When the Head Pro saw Nacs standing nearby smiling, he

immediately realized what had happened. Nacs had intentionally loosened the straps on Tuna's bag throughout the day and Tuna, being new to the game of golf, had just received his first golf lesson.

# 9. DOUBLE TROUBLE

A few years back a golf match was arranged with Nellie and Dash playing as partners, against Frankie and Knob. Nellie was about a 15 handicap; Frankie and Knob were both shitty golfers and were 28 handicappers. Dash played no more than twice a year but agreed to be Nellie's partner on this particular day. Dash did not have a handicap but would likely shoot about 110 on any given day.

Nellie did not know that Dash was a very inexperienced golfer and that it would be almost impossible for him to ever break 100. Nellie was led to believe that Dash was a 12 handicap.

Having the above information in hand, Nellie agreed that he and Dash would give Frankie and Knob one stroke per hole and the bet would be $1.00 per hole per person. Any team falling behind could bet "double or nothing" at any time.

Prior to making the above arrangements, Frankie, Dash, and Knob had met in private to work out the details. Nellie was totally in the dark as to Dash's true golfing ability, or lack thereof. It was agreed by Frankie, Dash, and Knob that no matter what happened, Nellie was not to be told that the match was a set up. Also, if Nellie and Dash got behind in the game, Dash was to urge Nellie to "double up" on the next hole in an effort to get Nellie's debt to the highest possible dollar figure. The three other golfers knew that Nellie would get big time pissed before the day was out, but agreed to move forward with the match anyway.

The match was set for a Friday afternoon at Downriver Golf Course in Spokane. Nellie arrived late; the other three contestants were waiting on the first tee box. Nellie was again reminded of the ground rules and he gladly agreed as he shook Dash's hand and said: "We are going to kick their ass". Game on.

Nellie, Frankie, and Knob, all hit decent drives off the first tee box. Dash swung hard at his ball, but lifted his head just before impact. The ball only moved about a foot off the tee. Dash commented: "I guess I should have hit some practice balls."

In the spirit of good sportsmanship, Frankie suggested that Dash "take a mulligan." Dash did just that and hit his mulligan deep into the trees off to the left side of the fairway. Nellie did not know Dash very well but when he saw Dash's performance on the first tee box, Nellie was a little concerned and wondered whether Dash was really a 12 handicap.

Dash was in and out of the trees the entire first hole and ended up with a nine. Nellie and Dash lost the hole and were down $1.00 each. On to the second hole.

Hole No. 2 is a straight away, downhill, par 3, about 175 yards in length. Trees line both sides of the hole but it is a wide fairway, and almost impossible to get into trouble. But Dash found trouble deep into the trees on the right side. By the time he found his way back, he had carded a six and he and his partner were down $2.00 each.

As he got ready to tee off on No. 3, Dash said to his partner: "Don't worry, I am always a slow starter. We will be fine". They went "double or nothing" on that hole.

Dash hit a nice drive down the middle of the fairway, about 240 yards out. Nellie breathed a sigh of relief.

On his second shot from about 130 yards out, Dash sliced an eight iron and the ball headed for the trees. It lodged in the "V" of a large pine tree at the juncture of where two large branches come together. It was about 8 feet off the ground. Nellie immediately suggested that Dash should be allowed a free drop onto the ground below. Frankie, an attorney and a man familiar with "rules", strongly responded by saying that Dash had two options: to hit it where it laid, or take an unplayable lie. Dash elected to play it---he reached up with his 3 iron and knocked the ball onto the ground---directly behind another tree. By the time Dash had recovered and played out the hole, he had recorded a seven, and he and Nellie were now down

$4.00 each.

Even though Dash had hit a good drive on 3, the way he played the rest of the hole gave Nellie cause to worry about the ability of his partner.

As the group headed to the 4th tee box, Dash assured Nellie that his worst golf was behind him. They doubled the bet on the 4th hole.

Dash actually played well on the par 4, 360-yard hole. But he missed a three-foot putt and took a six which cost them the hole. They were now down $8.00.

With a good hole under Dash's belt, Nellie had no trouble doubling up on the 5th hole, the No. 1 handicap hole on the course. There are trees on both sides of the 430-yard hole. But Nellie knew that Frankie and Knob, who both were 28 handicappers, would be hard pressed to get less than a six on the hole, and could very easily get a seven or an eight. Nellie would get either a par or a five at worst, and Dash would get nothing higher than a six. Nellie said: "We are doubling up here".

Frankie and Knob both hit straight drives but they were no more than 165 yards. Nellie smacked a 250-yard drive splitting the fairway. Dash pulled his drive onto number 4 fairway. He would have to go over the trees to get back to number 5 fairway. Nellie suggested that he chip his ball back to the 5th fairway rather than taking the aggressive approach over the trees. Dash said: "No, Nellie, I've got this shot". He pulled out his 4 iron and hit a solid shot, but the ball caught the top of the trees dropping straight down. Dash had no shot and now had to chip out to the 5th fairway. He was now laying three. The other three golfers in the foursome moved their respective balls up the fairway in uneventful fashion.

Dash was still about 200 yards short of the green. Nellie told Dash that he needed to get down in three more shots and they would win the hole. Nellie suggested that Dash hit a little five iron just in front of the green, chip up, and one putt for a six. Dash answered by saying: "I have a four hybrid that I have really been hitting good lately. I think I can make it".

Dash swung the 4 hybrid and hit the ball on the toe of the club sending it far into the trees off of the left side of the fairway. It took Dash two more strokes to get out of the trees. Dash ended up taking an eight on the hole and he and his partner were now down $16.00 each. Nellie was pissed.

The 6th hole at Downriver is about 130 yards slightly downhill. If the tee shot is pulled to the left, it will go down a steep ravine and cause nothing but trouble. Keep the ball right and everything is fine.

As they approached number 6 tee box, Dash turned to Nellie and said: "Par threes are my strong suit. I like this hole. We gotta double up here". Nellie asked: "Are you sure? If we lose this hole, we will be down $32.00". Dash said: "Its money in the bank".

Believe it or not, all four golfers hit the green with their tee shots. And all four two putted for pars. However, with the stroke that Frankie and his partner received, they won the hole and were now up $32.00.

The 7th hole is a long, 500 yard, uphill, par 5. Nellie had a six on the hole and the other three had sevens. With the extra stroke, Frankie and Knob again tied the hole.

The result on hole number 8 was much like hole number 7---with the stroke, the two teams again tied. On both hole number 7 and hole number 8, Nellie and Dash had doubled the bet, but no money changed hands because of the ties.

Hole number 9 is 330 yards uphill. One of the easiest holes on the course. Dash again urged Nellie to double the bet and he did. Nellie and Frankie both scored fives on the hole; Knob got a six; and Dash hit his ball into the sand trap next to the green. It took him two swings to get out and he also took a six on the hole. With the handicap stroke, Frankie and partner won the hole and were now up $64.00 each.

By the end of the 9th hole, Nellie was very upset with his playing partner. He asked: "Dash, are you really a twelve handicap?" Dash said: "I was last year but I haven't played a whole lot this season. But I really think I will do much better on the back nine".

Before teeing off on the back nine, Nellie approached Frankie and said: "There is no way Dash is a twelve handicap. Let's play the back even up so that we at least have a chance to get our money back". Frankie responded by saying: "Listen Nellie, a deal is a deal; we can't be changing the game at mid-point just because your guy had a couple of bad holes".

The game proceeded.

As the back nine progressed, Nellie refused to double up on some of the holes. In fact, had they doubled up on number 12, a hole that he and Dash won, the match would have been even.

But as fate would have it, Dash convinced Nellie to double up on number sixteen, a short par three hole, and on number eighteen. They lost both of those holes with Dash playing poorly on both.

The final tally was that Nellie and Dash lost $256.00 each. Nellie was livid.

After unloading their clubs, the boys decided to head to the Maxwell House Restaurant and Bar located a couple of miles away, to "square up" and have a beer.

After the four sat down at the table, Nellie, still very upset at his playing partner, turned to Dash and said: "There is no f---ing way you are a twelve handicap. Where did you establish your handicap—at Pine Acres (which is a par three course on Spokane's north side)"? Dash, not wanting to get into an argument, just ignored the question.

Nellie then pulled out his checkbook and asked: "Okay you prick, how much do we owe you"? Frankie said "You owe $256.00 each".

Nellie said: "Okay I will write my check to Frankie. Dash, why don't you pay Knob?"

Dash replied: "Nellie, I'm a little short today, would you mind paying Knob also and I will pay you back next week on pay day"?

This request to Nellie that he also pay Dash's gambling debt, was the last straw for Nellie. He stood up, madder than hell, and said to Dash:

"What in hell is your problem? First you tell me that you are a 12 handicap and then you play like shit, and cause me to lose $256.00, and now you ask me to also pay the $256.00 that you owe. Why don't you jam it up your ass? You shouldn't be gambling if you are such a shitty golfer".

Only then was Nellie informed that the match had been a "set-up" and he didn't owe a thing. The other three golfers had a good chuckle. Nellie smiled for the first time in 5 hours and said: "You bastards---why would you do that to a friend? You can't trust anybody anymore".

# 10. THE MISSING MONEY POUCH

Several years ago, the 24-man golf squad made a three-day summer golf trip into Eastern British Columbia. The group left Spokane early one Friday morning and played a round of golf at the Creston Golf Course, one at Kokanee Springs Golf Course, and the final round at Trickle Creek Golf Course near Kimberely. The crew headed home late Sunday afternoon.

As was customary procedure, Nellie made all the travel and golf arrangements. He booked the hotels, golf courses, and bus, with his personal credit card. Some of the guys would pay Nellie their share of the costs a week or two before the crew left on the trip. However, there were always a few "stragglers" who did not pay Nellie until they boarded the bus. Consequently, Nellie would always have a little satchel that he carried with him that would contain $5000.00 or $6000.00 in cash. Nellie carried it everywhere he went.

There were occasions during a trip that the boys would "steal" Nellie's satchel when he put it down for a minute to take care of the other errands that he was required to do because he was the trip organizer. Nellie would bitch and moan until his satchel was returned to him.

On this particular trip to eastern British Columbia, the crew had finished its three rounds of golf and was on its way back to Spokane on Sunday afternoon. The bus needed to go through customs at the Eastport border crossing in order to reenter the United States.

There is a Duty-Free Store located just a mile or so before hitting the Eastport border crossing. Booze is about half price at the Duty Free and most of the guys buy a couple of bottles to take back to Spokane.

On this particular Sunday, the bus stopped as usual at the Duty-Free Store. All the guys went in, bought their booze, and returned to the bus.

The bus then headed towards the border. The bus stopped and cleared customs at Eastport and headed down the road towards Spokane.

The bus had traveled about 20 miles down the road after leaving the border crossing. The guys were nicely settled in, some playing Stook and some just relaxing with a cold beer.

One of the card players asked Nellie to "change a hundred". Nellie said "no problem". He looked for his satchel---it was nowhere to be found. After a few minutes of searching Nellie said: "Okay— which one of you jackasses has got my money pouch?

Several more minutes passed but there was no satchel.

Finally, everyone realized that the satchel was not on the bus.

"Bussy---turn this bus around," shouted Nellie. "I think I might have left the satchel at the Duty-Free Store".

The Bussy found a place to turn around and headed back to the border. There was close to $6000.00 cash in the satchel and Nellie was "scared shitless" that the satchel, and the money, were long gone.

It seemed like an eternity to Nellie as the bus covered those twenty miles back to the border.

As the Bussy brought his bus to a stop at the drive through area of the Canadian border, the Border Agent working the window said: "I was expecting you. Are you looking for this"? The Agent handed the money pouch to the bus driver through the open window and said: "You really should take better care of your money. The cashier at the Duty-Free Store brought this to me and said you would probably be back for it".

Nellie looked inside the satchel---all the money was still there. He let out a yell and said: "The drinks are on me when we hit Sandpoint".

We did---and they were.

This story had a happy ending, but the boys never let Nellie forget what a shitty "banker" he was.

# 11. MEN AT WORK

I t was a hot Friday evening in Whitefish, Montana. The guys, 22 strong, had just finished a round of golf at the Whitefish Golf and Country Club. And they were thirsty. They stopped at the Bulldog Tavern to have a cold one while they waited for their two remaining golfers from Calgary to rendezvous with them.

• This was the first golf trip to Montana for Doughber and Burgey. Both of them had spent considerable time in Spokane over the years and knew most of the 22 guys who had rode the bus over from Spokane.

It was just getting dark when the bar room door opened. The bar was jammed and noisy.

A man walked in wearing golf shorts and an ugly striped tee shirt. He was followed by another man wearing a black cowboy hat. Sticking out of the back of the first man's ugly tee shirt, and extending above his head, was a yellow highway sign which said in black letters "MEN WORKING AHEAD".

The Doughber had arrived and Burgey was riding shotgun.

# 12. A FASHION STATEMENT

When the Doughburr was young, it was obvious that he was different. He had a tough time with "color schemes" and matching a shirt with a pair of pants. Although he was exceptionally bright, having graduated number one in his University CPA class, no one ever accused him of being a fashion leader.

And so, it came as no surprise when the guy working the Pro Shop at the Eagle Bend Golf Course in Big Fork, Montana, said to him: "We will make an exception for you today, but in the future, you will need to dress appropriately in order to play on this golf course".

To set the scene, starting at the head and working to the feet: Doughburr was wearing a jungle safari hat; the two lenses in his sunglasses were each a little larger than a silver dollar; his leather necklace was imbedded with some type of animal teeth; his yellow tee shirt was lined with horizontal stripes; he was wearing a pair of checkered shorts; his socks were white in color and extended almost to the knees; and he was wearing black oxfords.

His golf bag was red in color and was one of those "starter" bags like the ones that are given to young children when they are just starting to play golf in the back yard.

His bag did not have a shoulder strap but only a handle.

The bag contained four clubs---an old wooden driver, a three iron, a five iron, and a blade putter.

Doughburr made many trips to Montana with the guys and each day his attire was "unusual". He certainly kept the boys entertained and the Pro Shops on their toes.

# 13. JUST FOLLOW THE CHICKEN BONES

I t was that time of year again---the second weekend in August was just a week away. The 24 golfers would be hauling ass for Montana where they would spend 3 days golfing and socializing, just like they had every year for the past fifteen.

Freddy, the guy in charge of providing "snacks" for the three-day bus trip, had a quandary on his hands: how do I get the right food to keep most of the 24 guys happy---some of the boys are sure to bitch no matter what I get. In prior years Freddy had tried everything from potato chips, to pepperoni, to pickled eggs, to "Hot Mama's". Sometimes the boys liked his choices but some of the guys were never happy.

As he was finishing his lunch one day at the Maxwell House Restaurant, he got to talking to Ricardo, the owner of the Maxwell House. He explained his dilemma about the food for the boys and asked Ricardo if he had any ideas as to how to keep 24 party boys happy for three days. Ricardo immediately said "fried chicken. Everybody likes chicken even when it's cold. And it is will keep for three days---just put a couple of ice bags on top and you're good to go".

"Great idea" said Freddy, "can you fix us up"?

"Absolutely" said Ricardo. "How many pieces do you want. I can fry them up the night before your trip and have them ready for you on Friday morning just before you leave".

"We have 24 guys---so how about 200 pieces. I will stop by on Friday morning and pick them up and pay you then".

"I will have them ready to go on Friday morning," said Ricardo.

When Friday rolled around, Freddy picked up the chicken and delivered the 200 pieces to the bus. It didn't take long for the boys to dig in. "Great idea Freddy, after all these years you finally figured it out," said the boys. They seemed pleased with Freddy's work. Freddy smiled—he was so proud of his accomplishment, as small as it was.

Eagle Bend Golf Course is a beautiful golf course located at Bigfork, Montana. It is located about 250 miles from Spokane. The bus pulled in just in time to meet the 2:30 PM tee time. The boys divided into their pre-arranged foursomes and started out. There was always a lot of game "action" among the guys.

Rollie was the oldest guy on the trip. He was sometimes referred to as "Gramps". He was a "veteran" so far as the Montana Golf trip was concerned. He had only missed the trip a couple of times since it first started some fifteen years earlier.

The boys knew that Rollie's patience was wearing a little thin when it came to some of the antics of the younger guys. And it wasn't beyond the younger guys to take a dig or two at the older fellows, especially if they knew they could get a reaction.

And so, it was as the boys teed off at Eagle Bend that day.

Some of the guys decided to take a few pieces of the fried chicken with them on their carts just in case they got a little hungry during the golf match. One foursome of younger guys carried a large batch of chicken with them as they teed off just in front of Rollie's foursome. They were also well stocked with cold Kokenee beer.

At the 14th hole, a couple of members of this younger foursome, DJ and Red, started snacking on the chicken. They finished hole 14 and headed to No. 15.

When Rollie and his foursome arrived at the 14th green and prepared to putt out, Rollie discovered that the hole was surrounded by chicken bones, all nicely laid out in a circle about a foot in diameter, making it impossible to access the hole without clearing away the bones. Rollie undertook the task of clearing the bones away so his group could putt out. He used some profanities as he described the "childly" behavior of the "kids" in the four some ahead.

Rollie's group then played on and headed to the 15<sup>th</sup> green. When they arrived at the 15<sup>th</sup> green, they found more chicken bones—this time the bones were stuck in the green standing on end and once again surrounded the hole. Rollie had struggled all day with his game and was already in a fowl frame of mind as he again cleared away the chicken bones. He yelled to the "kids" ahead: "Why don't you grow up you assholes". Loud chuckles came from the foursome ahead---they knew they had hit a nerve.

Rollie's group headed towards the 16<sup>th</sup> green. The foursome ahead was very noisy and seemed to be having a good time. The Kokanees had obviously kicked in. Rollie was already pissed because he was having a bad golf day and the chicken bones on the 14th and 15th greens just made the situation all that much worse

When he and his group arrived at the 16<sup>th</sup> green, Rollie saw the name "Rollie" spelled out in chicken bones right in front of the cup. His three playing partners started laughing and couldn't stop. Rollie lost it. He threw his putter and it went over a barbed wire fence that acted as a boundary fence off to the right side of the green. The group in front were laughing historically---they were getting the reaction they had hoped for from "Gramps".

In order to finish hole 16, Rollie had to climb over the barbed wire fence, retrieve his putter, return to the green, and then putt out. Everyone but Rollie was laughing as he putted out on 16. Rollie thought he had seen the last of the chicken bones. But as he putted his ball straight towards the cup on the 17<sup>th</sup> green, his ball hit the center of the cup but stayed out. The hole was full of chicken bones.

The boys in front were breaking a gut; Rollie's own group couldn't contain themselves. Rollie yelled at the group ahead and called them the "three Stooges" even though there were four of them.

The 18<sup>th</sup> hole was uneventful; the boys ahead had run out of chicken.

After getting a couple of drinks in the Clubhouse, Rollie eventually settled down and even chuckled a little knowing that the "kids" had got to "Gramps".

# 14. "WHERE ARE MY CLUBS?"

Buffalo Hills Golf Course is located in the middle of Kalispel, Montana. It has one of the most beautiful log clubhouses in the country. The golf course is very hilly and is a true test for any golfer.

The 4th hole is a fairly short par four. It has a substantially elevated tee box. The golfer hits to a beautiful valley below, with both sides of the fairway lined with trees. At the bottom of the valley, the hole makes a sharp dogleg to the left. Good golfers have to use less than driver off the tee box to avoid going through the fairway and into the trees.

One Saturday morning Rollie's foursome had just arrived at No. 4 tee box. There was a group in front of them teeing off. There was a short wait of probably five minutes before Rollie's foursome could tee off.

Many years before, Rollie had been awarded a set of golf clubs for being the first star in a hockey game while he was playing for the Chicago Black Hawks. The set of clubs came with a bright green golf bag---the only one of its kind that anybody had ever seen. It stood out like a hooker in a convent. But Rollie loved it and, despite many negative comments about it, he refused to replace the bag.

On this particular day, by the time Rollie's group gained the tee box, another Spokane foursome had pulled up behind their golf carts. While Rollie and his playing partner teed off, Lunker undid the straps to their two golf bags. Rollie and his partner hit nice drives right down the middle of the fairway to the valley down below. They were both smiling and in the best of moods as they got into their cart and made their way down into the valley to hit their second shots.

Just as they pulled away from the tee box, their two bags fell off scattering their clubs all over the hillside. Neither Rollie nor his partner heard the bags hit the ground.

Their cart pulled up to Rollie's ball down in the valley. Rollie, the cart driver, got out of the cart, walked to the rear of the cart to get an iron out of his ugly green bag for his second shot, and lo and behold, the cart was devoid of bags and clubs. Rollie and his cart partner looked back up the hill towards the tee box and saw their bags and clubs scattered across the hillside.

Back into the cart they got, turned the cart around, and headed back up to the tee box. They were pissed. When they arrived at the tee box, Rollie said: "you childish bastards, that's not even funny". The gut-wrenching laughs coming from the bellies of the next foursome made it clear that not everyone agreed with Rollie's comment.

# 15. STREAKER

The Polson, Montana Golf Course is located about 35 miles from Kalispel. The bus passes right by the course on the way into Kalispel. By the time the bus arrived in Polson, the guys had already been riding for about 4 hours and were getting a little antsy. Polson seemed like a good place to play the first round of golf on this 3-day Montana trip.

It was about 2:00 PM on that Friday and it was exceptionally hot with temperatures in the mid-90s. The 24 guys unloaded their clubs and made their way to the driving range to hit a few balls before teeing off.

Frankie was along on the trip. He was in his late 50s, and was a little overweight. He stood about 5 feet 9 inches tall and tipped the scales at about 235 pounds. He smoked cigars continuously, one after the other. In fact, when Frankie would go into a restaurant or grocery store where smoking was not allowed, Frankie would snuff out the cigar and lay it on a window ledge outside the store while he ate or did his shopping. When he exited the building he would grab his cigar off the window ledge, light it up again, and continue puffing.

Frankie looks like a character out of Damon Runyon. He regularly wears suspenders and no one can ever remember seeing him wearing a belt. He was the only one of the 24 golfers to not wear short pants that day. He never wore shorts when he golfed—only wrinkled dress pants. And he never wore typical golf shirts---usually long-sleeved dress shirts that buttoned up the front. He was the worst dressed guy on the bus that day and even when he "dressed up" his clothes looked horrible.

Frankie was always in a good mood and he was always smiling. He was fun to be around and everyone loved him.

So far as his golfing ability was concerned, Frankie was the shits. He rarely broke a hundred. But he sure had fun.

The first foursome teed off and started its journey down the first fairway. Frankie was in the second group that day and was the cart partner of Judge Johnny. After playing the first four holes, Frankie complained about how hot it was and said he wished he had brought some golf shorts. After playing a couple more holes, Frankie said: "screw it-- I have to get out of these pants". Right there, on the seventh tee box, Frankie took his pants off and threw them in the basket of the golf cart. He played the rest of the round in his white briefs---except the briefs were not entirely white, there was a brown streak of some kind on the back end of the undies. It never bothered Frankie, not even a little bit, not even when he approached the young lady driving the refreshment cart to buy a round of beer.

After completing the 18$^{th}$ hole, Frankie slid back into his pants just like it was a normal day.

# 16. "BOOM!"

The back nine of the Polson golf course is heavily treed. If you slice or hook the ball, you will be in for a long afternoon.

It was a warm Friday afternoon when cart partners, Lunker and Lefty, drove away from the first tee box. But before heading towards their drives, they made a pit stop at the bus to load up their beer cooler with about 24 Kokanees. That would usually be enough to get them through the round, unless some of the other guys "stole" some of the beer.

It was the 15th hole. Lunker and Lefty had just hit their drives. Lefty had pulled his tee shot into the trees just off the fairway on the left side. Lunker was down the middle. As they made their way towards Lefty's ball, DJ came driving over from the adjoining fairway. He asked: "Can you guys spare a couple of beers; we are completely out"? Lefty replied: "No, we only have four left and that has to do us for the rest of the round". Despite that answer, DJ got out of his cart and approached Lefty's cart intent on "stealing" a couple of beers. Realizing that DJ's intentions were not good, Lefty jumped on the accelerator and the cart took off. It just so happened that Lefty's cart was on a steep downhill grade and the cart sped up in a hurry. As he pulled away, Lefty was looking back over his shoulder as DJ started running towards the cart intent on grabbing a couple of beers. All of a sudden "BOOM"---Lefty's cart had smashed head on into a huge fir tree. Lunker was thrown out and over the front of the cart and landed on the ground, narrowly missing the tree. The sound from the impact was heard all over the course. A huge dent was left in the front bumper of the cart and the steering wheel was bent.

DJ never got the beer.

After completing their round, Lefty and Lunker parked their cart on the side of the clubhouse and the bus headed into Kalispel. They never heard from the Pro shop.

# 17. EARLY MORNING WAKE UP

I t seems like the first night on the town in Kalispel is always eventful. The boys have been looking forward to getting out of town and doing a little "socializing".

On this particular trip into Montana, the boys were booked into the Motel 6 just off the main drag in Kalispel. The Motel was a "Plain Janer"; it didn't have a coffee shop, meeting rooms, or any other amenities, just cheap rooms and a perfect set up for these 24 golfers.

As was customary, the guys had closed down the bars and then went to the only restaurant in town that was still open at 2:00 AM. They chowed down and finally got back to their rooms at about 3:30 AM. They had an 11:00 o'clock tee time the next morning.

Kenny, the bus driver, already had four hours of sleep under his belt by the time the boys returned to their rooms.

Coxy, never one to pass up a good opportunity, picked up his room phone and called Kenny. When Kenny answered, Coxy said: "Mr. Wilson, this is the front desk. I hate to bother you at such an hour as this, but I just realized that your bus is parked in front of the Motel. We have a large wedding party coming in here for a reception at 9:00 AM tomorrow. Could I impose upon you to move your bus around to the back of the building"?

Kenny, still half asleep, answered: "No problem. I will get right on it".

At about 9:30 the next morning, the boys boarded the bus at the rear of the Motel. As he was getting on the bus, Coxy asked Kenny: "Kenny, I thought you parked the bus out front last night. What's the bus doing back here"?

Kenny replied: "I got a call from the front desk about 3:00 AM this morning, telling me they had a large party coming to the Motel this morning for a wedding reception. So, I had to move the bus around back".

Coxy responded: "That's interesting, because I have never seen a restaurant or banquet rooms here".

Kenny thought for a moment and, realizing that he had been the victim of an early morning prank, said: "You little Prick, Coxy".

# 18. WHERE'S MY CAR?

I t was a typical hot July Saturday in Spokane, WA. A group of eight guys decided to play an early morning round of golf at Wandermere Golf Course located on the north end of the city limits. The crew met at the golf course restaurant at 8 am to have a quick snack and divide into two foursomes. As always, the guys asked each player for his handicap number---the answers were usually a little inflated but that was just normal for this group. Plus, if anyone was too far off his "correct" handicap number, and won money because of it, there were always ways of dealing with that at a later time.

On this particular morning the Big Guy declared himself to be an 18 handicap even though it was not unusual for him to shoot in the low to mid-eighties. On this morning, to justify his "18" declaration, he declared "I have only played once in the past six weeks and the last time I played I shot a 93". The hooters called "bullshit" but nevertheless put the Big Guy down for an 18 handicap.

Now there is a reason for the name "Big Guy". His body size is as big as his declared handicap. He stands about six feet one inch and tips the scales at about 300 big ones. Nonetheless he has been a very popular member of this golf group for many years and a regular on the Montana Golf Trip.

The individual and team games were set with each player throwing $40.00 in the pot to be paid out to the winners at the end of the match.

At 9 AM the guys were off and running. For the first nine holes, everything was pretty uneventful except for the fact that the Big Guy shot a 39 on the front. The wolves were already starting to howl.

Play continued and the back nine was completed. The guys all made their way into the lounge to have a beer and calculate the individual and team payouts. Usually, the guy that wins most of the dough, buys the beers. Just good sportsmanship.

Wouldn't you know it---the Big Guy "had his best round in three years---I just can't believe how well I played today and I got really lucky on some putts". His 18-hole score was 80.

The guys had heard this broken record before and were not too happy. When the payouts were made the Big Guy received exactly half of the entire pot---$160.00.

The group's response to the Big Guy's winnings was "You are picking up the beer tab today". The Big Guy responded by saying "Sorry boys, I have a ton of yard work to do this afternoon and I need to be going. I need to stop at Lowes and get some yard supplies and then I am heading back to my house to get my chores done. But I want to thank you all for the donation and let's do this again real soon".

With that explanation the Big Guy was out the door. The remaining seven golfers were pissed. When a member of the group upsets the other members, and especially under these types of circumstances, imaginations go to work. And it didn't take long in this case.

Lefty was one of the groups of eight playing golf on this Saturday. He has a body repair shop and repossession business in north Spokane which includes three tow trucks. The shop is located about a mile from the Lowes hardware store where the Big Guy said he was stopping to pick up yard supplies. Lefty said "I am going to have a little fun with the Big Guy's car and let him know that he is not an eighteen-handicap golfer". With that comment, Lefty was out the door.

Back then, the Big Guy drove a bright green colored SUV that was easy to spot.

Lefty immediately headed to his body repair shop, got one of his tow trucks, and then headed for the Lowe's parking lot. He had no trouble spotting the Big Guy's car. With many years of experience doing car repossessions for various Spokane Banks, Lefty was soon hooked onto the Big Guy's car in a matter of minutes and was headed down the road, green car in tow.

A couple of miles to the south of Lowes hardware store is the Northtown Shopping Centre comprised of many different stores and shops. Northtown has a huge parking area with literally hundreds of cars parked, especially on a busy Saturday afternoon. Lefty soon realized that Northtown would be a perfect unloading area for a bright green SUV. He found an open spot and dropped off the Big Guy's SUV. The parking lot would be full of cars until nine o'clock that night and no one would think to look there for a missing vehicle. Mission accomplished!

Fast forward about one hour to the Lowes parking lot. Out of the doors comes a big man with his arms full of items. He takes a right turn heading towards the parking stall that he just recently parked his vehicle in. As he arrived at that stall, there was no green car. He thought to himself, maybe its further down the lot---so he walked further down the lot. Still no green car. Now he was thinking that maybe he misjudged where he had parked the car. So, he continued walking and looking---still no car. He spent the next 30 minutes walking all around the parking areas with no luck in finding his vehicle. Now he was getting desperate and was thinking that maybe his car has been stolen. Finally, he decided I better call the police and report the car as stolen.

The Big Guy got his cell phone out of his pocket and called the Spokane Police Department and explained the situation. He provided a description of his car but didn't know the license plate number. He provided his name, address, and phone number to the police dept and was told that they would send an officer out to the area within 30 minutes.

A police officer finally arrived at the Lowes parking area. The Big Guy met with the officer and gave him all the details. The officer said he would put out a BOLO (Be On The Look Out) for the Big Guy's vehicle. The police officer was kind enough to drive the Big Guy to his residence which was not far from the Lowes store.

During the next few hours, the Big Guy was thinking about contacting his insurance company to report the missing vehicle. But he decided to wait until Monday morning to see if by chance the vehicle might be found.

It was about 10 PM that evening when the Big Guy received a telephone call from the police department telling him that they had located his vehicle in the Northtown parking lot. The police officer said that they did not know how the vehicle got to the Northtown location but it appeared undamaged and the Big Guy was free to pick up the car whenever he wanted. The Big Guy got a friend to drive him to Northtown where he picked up his vehicle, undamaged.

The next morning, the Big Guy got on the phone and started calling the guys he had golfed with the day before. Even though they all denied knowing anything about a missing car, the Big Guy had a hunch that they knew more than they were telling him. Weeks passed and the Big Guy never learned how his vehicle had been taken from the Lowes parking lot and showed up at Northtown. Eventually he just dropped his attempt to get answers.

If the Big Guy happens to read this story, it will be the first time he has learned the details of his missing car. And hopefully he will have learned that he is not an eighteen handicap.

# 19. CASH CALL

Doughburr was a Certified Chartered Accountant. And so, it seemed that he would be the logical one to handle the "cash call" money.

The guys had a regular routine when they were on the Montana golf trips---when they went out on the town for a few drinks after golf, each guy would throw $25.00 in the pot for drinks and snacks. This fund would be handled by one of the guys who would pay for all the drinks and snacks. When the pot ran dry the money guy would yell "cash call" and the guys would anti up again.

Such was the case one Saturday night in a lively western bar in downtown Kalispel. The guys had each tossed $25.00 into the pot and Doughburr had been appointed the money manager.

The money manager had a lot of discretion in deciding whether to buy beer or hard drinks. On this particular night Doughburr decided to buy drinks rather than beer. And he decided that the drinks that he bought would be based upon the color of the drinks, not the type of alcohol that was in the drinks. Doughburr would watch the cocktail waitresses delivering drinks to other customers and would then tell the waitress "We need 22 of that one".

The first round of drinks were red in color. The boys drank them down with no problem. The second round was a green concoction of some kind---nobody really knew for sure what was in them. Again, the boys knocked them back. The third round was yellow in color and the fourth round was blue. And then Doughburr yelled "cash call". Four drinks and the "cash call" money of approximately $500.00 was gone.

There was some grumbling among the troops as they reached in their pockets for another $25.00, but everybody divvied up again.

After three or four more rounds of colored drinks, and with the "cash call" money again depleted, the boys called it a night.

A couple of the boys threw up that night and most had some degree of stomach problems the next day when they headed out to the golf course.

That was the only time that Doughburr was allowed to oversee the "cash call" money.

# 20. "MAN DOWN"

**M**eadow Lakes Golf Course is a beautiful track. It is located at Columbia Falls about 20 or so miles down the road from Kalispell. Every year the boys arrange to play this course.

One particular year a tall, slim, drink of water, named Monty rode down from Calgary with the Doughburr and joined the Spokane boys on their annual three-day golf outing. Monty was a Calgary businessman and a serious sort of guy. He had never before met any of the Spokane boys. Right from the start he appeared to be a little out of place.

One of the courses that the group played that year was Meadow Lakes, a course where every fairway is lined by trees. If you don't hit your drives straight, you are in for a long day.

Monty was in a foursome immediately ahead of DJ and Red. DJ plays golf one weekend per year---on the Montana golf outing. His golf ability could be accurately described as "poor". He and Red are good friends and often are cart partners. They both enjoy drinking beer during their rounds of golf---lots of beer.

On this particular day, DJ and Red were about half way through the back nine. Monty and his group were immediately ahead. Monty's drive had caught the trees just off the left side of the fairway. He was addressing his ball for his second shot. Not seeing Monty in the trees, DJ hit his tee shot and it hooked into the trees on the left side of the fairway, striking Monty on the forehead. Monty fell to the ground, out cold. Red and the other members of DJ's foursome saw what happened and raced to Monty's side. When they got to Monty, Red yelled: "man down, man down". The guys applied some ice from their beer cooler to Monty's forehead and he soon came around. After a few minutes he seemed to be okay and he finished the last few holes.

In the clubhouse after golf, all the guys gathered to square up their bets and have a beer. Monty had a knot on his forehead the size of a .... well, the size of a golf ball!

Monty never made the Montana trip again.

# 21. JUDGE JOHNNY'S BILLBOARD
## --- FIRST EDITION

He stands 5 feet 5 inches tall---if you measure from the bottom of the curb. He tips the scales at 215 pounds---if you weigh him after he has done his morning constitutional. He has a hair do that looks so much like Ben Franklin's that some of the boys call him "Ben". His legs are so short that the legs of normal golf shorts hang well below his knees leaving only six inches between the top of his socks and the bottom of his shorts. His head is larger than average, so much so that golf hats out of the Pro Shop won't fit his noggin. He always wore white running shoes when he golfed---never golf spikes. He is a chain smoker when he golfs---one after another for 18 holes. And with the advent of the cell phone with camera attachment, there is no shortage of photos of The Judge in his various attires.

Judge Johnny gets his name honestly. He was a District Court judge in Spokane for ten years until he was dethroned in a costly election several years back. Since then, he has practiced law in Spokane as a criminal defense lawyer and he is one of the best in town. He likes it when people call him "Judge"---it makes him feel important.

In 30 years, the Judge has only missed two of the trips into Montana.

The Judge is a bad golfer---he claims to be a 22 handicap, but that is just his ego talking---he is more like a 29 handicap. But he is always willing to make a bet or two with the guys when he tees it up in Montana.

Due to the fact that the Judge inflates his golfing abilities, every guy on the Montana trip wants to have a game with him. He is known as "Easy Pickens", the brother of "Slim". He is a regular payer and a good guy to know if you are a little short of cash.

The guys had just spent three days in Montana and were on their way home. It was approaching midnight as the bus wound its way through the 4th of July pass heading towards Spokane. The topic of conversation over the Stook game turned to the Judge who was sound asleep, and snoring, in one of the front seats.

"What do you guys think of getting a billboard made for the Judge. We have some good photos of him and could figure out something nice to say on the billboard so it would look real professional. We will make sure to get a billboard that is on a busy street so it gets lots of viewers. The Judge would really like that".

It was a great idea that the guys had come up with and they would check with a billboard company the following week and report back to the guys.

After meeting with the billboard company, it was determined that the cost for the billboard for a one-month period of time, at a busy location, would be about $1000.00. Immediately there were ten guys that offered to throw in $100.00 each.

And so it came to be. The Judge would have his very own billboard advertisement. The photo would be a full body shot showing him in his normal golf attire, with about six inches of his legs showing, no hat, and white sneakers. The photo selected would show the Judge in his "follow-through" stance, just after he had played a shot. It was a superb photo.

Contributions from the guys quickly flowed in. After another meeting with the billboard company the details were worked out. The billboard advertisement would read:

HEEEERES JOHNNY!!

Golf Lessons Cheap

By (Judge's Full Name Here)

Call: 509-701-XXXX (The Judge's real cell phone number)

One third of the billboard would be taken up with the Judge's photo.

It was decided to place the billboard on Northwest Boulevard, near Monroe Street, which is a heavily traveled arterial in Spokane. It would run for 30 days. The Judge would be so proud.

The billboard first appeared on a Monday morning. Of course, The Judge knew nothing about it.

It just so happened that the Judge had to appear in Spokane County Superior Court (he was no longer a sitting judge at the time) for "docket call" at 9:00 AM the next day. "Docket Call" is where many attorneys appear in the courtroom of the presiding judge to see whether their particular case will be assigned out that day to another courtroom for trial.

On this particular morning, the presiding judge came out from his chambers and took his seat on the bench as is customary. He looked out into the courtroom and saw fifty or so lawyers seated and waiting to hear whether their cases would be assigned out. He saw Judge Johnny sitting in the courtroom and, before he started assigning cases, the presiding judge said: "Mr. (Judge Johnny's last name), have you changed occupations? I understand you are now in the business of giving golf lessons."

Judge Johnny got up and said: "I am not sure what you are referring to, Your Honor".

Presiding Judge: "I was on my way to work this morning when I noticed your billboard advertising golf lessons. I hope my court assignment for you this morning won't affect your new business".

The courtroom of attorneys erupted in laughter. Even though they had not seen the billboard, they knew something very unusual was happening.

During the lunch hour that day, Judge Johnny drove out to Northwest Blvd and saw his billboard advertisement for the first time. He was so proud.

PS: Over the next 30 days, Judge Johnny received numerous telephone calls, some serious and some not, requesting information about his golf lessons. He received one call from a person claiming to be part of a group of 30 Chinese high school students visiting Spokane for a week, inquiring as to whether The Judge would also supply, free of charge, the golf clubs necessary to take his free lessons.

# 22. JUDGE JOHNNY'S BILLBOARD
## --- SECOND EDITION

It had been 10 years since The Judge had run his first billboard advertisement. It was such a success that the boys thought it might be time for a sequel.

It was early August and the annual three-day golfing excursion to Whitefish, Montana, was just a week away. The Judge would need some clothes.

A trip to the Goodwill store in downtown Spokane was the starting place. A nice pair of colorful shorts with a 42-inch waist was at the top of the shopping list. The lady clerk quickly gave directions to the proper area of the store. It wasn't long before a lovely green fatigue pair of shorts, proper waist size and all, was discovered and purchased for $3.00.

As the bus pulled out of Spokane early that next Friday morning, The Judge was asked to step up to the front of the bus where he was presented with a belated birthday present---the $3.00 pair of shorts. He was very happy that the other 23 guys on the bus felt so highly of him that they would make a contribution towards his new $3.00 shorts. Life couldn't be much better.

The Judge was encouraged to wear his new shorts for the Saturday round of golf at the Whitefish Golf and Country Club. He willingly obliged---The Judge was always such a good sport.

The bottoms of the shorts hung down well below The Judge's knees, almost touching his white socks. Not much leg skin showing on this day.

The Judge wore a bright orange golf shirt which seemed to clash a little with the green fatigue shorts, but even on his best days The Judge was not much of a fashion statement. His attire really wasn't too far off his norm.

As The Judge hit his practice balls on the driving range that morning, several action shots were taken of the 5-foot 5-inch Judge as he made his way through his warm up routine.

The trip ended uneventfully and the guys made their way back to Spokane.

A week or so passed since the group had returned to Spokane. The phone rang. It was the billboard company calling: "Can you come on down to the office and finalize the details for The Judge's new billboard"?

Before the day was over the details for the new billboard were set. It would read:

LEGS, BELLYS & BALLS

Free Golf Lessons

CALL JOHN (LAST NAME HERE)

509-801-xxxx (Available seven days a week)

The billboard advertisement would again run for 30 days. It would be placed on Division Street, about 2 blocks south of Francis Ave. Division Street is the busiest arterial in the City of Spokane. Once again, the billboard would have a life-sized picture of The Judge but this time, he would be depicted in his bright orange golf shirt and green fatigue shorts. The cost would be $1150.00. Again, there was no shortage of contributors.

And so, it ran for 30 days.

The Judge's phone started to ring. He received a call from Channel 6 TV station wanting to do an interview. He received a call from Doug Clark, columnist for the Spokesman-Review, the only daily newspaper in Spokane. He also received many calls from golfers looking for help with their golf games. And with the lessons being free, what better bargain could a person find?

The Judge was the happiest guy in town. He loved the publicity and granted all interview requests. The TV station did a three minute take on him; the Spokesman-Review wrote a huge article on him, and included a picture of The Judge standing under the billboard holding a golf club and grinning from ear to ear.

And the guys who contributed to the cost of the billboard: they all said that it was the best money they had ever spent.

# 23. RAIN GEAR FOR SALE

Prairie Falls Golf Course is located about 20 miles east of Spokane, just across the Washington border, in the State of Idaho.

One Saturday, four of the Spokane guys decided to drive out to Prairie Falls and play a round of golf.

It was a nice July day. The sun was shining and a nice breeze was blowing. Perfect golf conditions.

The guys had played an uneventful first eight holes and had just teed off on number nine. As the group made its way towards their second shots, the Judge felt some water on his face and he immediately knew that he was going to get rained on and he had forgot to bring any rain gear.

At the turn, the Judge went into the Pro Shop and bought a full set of rain gear, both the jacket and the pants, and pulled the gear on over his regular golf attire.

The foursome teed off on the tenth hole and played the back nine without any problems.

The Judge was the only one on the course that day wearing rain gear. The sun was shining. The other guys said: "Why the rain gear"? Judge said he had got rained on when playing hole nine. The guys looked at him kinda funny, and then looked over at the ninth fairway where the sprinkler system was watering the fairway. Judge had spent close to $100 for rain gear.

Even till this day, Judge still gets reminded of his "buy" at the Prairie Falls Pro Shop.

# 24. DOUBLE UP

They had just completed the front nine at Downriver Golf Course, a course down by the Spokane River which had been cut out of the trees many years before. They were exactly even at the turn.

Nacs and Knob going toe to toe, $5.00 per hole. Nacs had to give Knob one stroke per hole except on the par threes, and had to give Knob an extra stoke on the 18th hole just in case Knob was behind and needed to double up. Nacs was a far better golfer than the Knob.

The betting was simple: each hole was worth $5.00. When a player was behind, he could double the value of the next hole if he so desired, but he was not required to double up if he did not want to.

They teed off on number 10. Nacs sliced his ball onto the road on the right side and out of bounds. He lost that hole and was down $5.00.

On hole 11, Nacs hit another bad drive, this one over by the maintenance shed. He had to chip out and he could not recover. Down $10.00.

Hole number 12 is a long, 220-yard par three. Nacs did not have to give a stroke here so he doubled up again. Nacs had a 5 and Knob had a four. Nacs was now down $20.00.

Number 13 is a 500-yard par five hole. Perfect for Nacs because he hits the ball so much further than Knob. A sure win. "You are doubled here Knob".

Nacs' drive hit a tree on the left side of the fairway, and bounded into the forest. By the time he was done in the trees, Nacs had scored a seven to Knob's six. Nacs was now down $40.00.

The 14th hole is another par 5 but not quite as long as 13. Nacs knew that even with his stroke, Knob could never beat Nacs on two straight par 5s. "I am doubling up here" said Nacs.

Unbelievably, Knob parred the hole as did Nacs, but with his stroke, Knob won again. Nacs was now down $80.00.

The 15th hole is an uphill and rather short par 4. Nacs, now showing a few nerves, and not being the usual cocky and carefree guy the boys had grown accustomed to playing golf with, said "I got you here", meaning that he was again doubling up.

On the left side of the 15th fairway sits a large old fir tree. The tee shot needs to be to the right of that tree in order to have a short iron into the green. Nacs hit a great drive but unfortunately his ball caught a branch of that old fir tree and ricocheted deep into the trees off to the left of the fairway. Again, he had to waste a shot in order to get back on the fairway. Both he and Knob scored fives on the hole and with his stroke, Knob won the hole. Nacs was now down $160.00.

Number 16 at Downriver is a straight away par 3 stretching about 165 yards. Other than some over- hanging tree branches on the right side of the fairway, the hole is a pretty easy par 3.

Nacs did not have to give a stroke here and immediately said: "I got ya".

Knob hit his best drive of the day and found the front edge of the green. Nac's drive caught the over-hanging tree branches on the right, dropping his ball straight down. He chipped up and two putted for a bogey. Knob had an easy two putt for a par. Nacs was now down $320.00 with two holes to play.

The 17th hole is a very short 315-yard par four. Even the high handicap golfers can reach the green in two. And that is exactly what Knob did after first learning that Nacs was doubling up. They both had pars on the hole and Nacs was now down $640.00 going home.

Before they teed off on 18, Nacs asked Knob: "would you be willing to only take one stroke here because I am down to you"? "You are my friend Nacs, why would I not do that for you" replied Knob.

"Alright I will then double you here" said Nacs.

Both guys made fives on number 18 and, with the stroke he had to give, Nacs was now in debt $1280.00.

The guys went into the Clubhouse to square up and have a beer. Nacs was bitching about having to give too many strokes. Knob was saying how lucky he had been and that he just "got some bounces today".

Nacs reached into his pocket and handed $45.00 to Knob saying: "here ya go you bastard. You gotta buy the beer". Knob looked at the $45.00 and asked: "what is this"? Nacs replied: "I lost all nine holes. At $5.00 per hole that is $45.00". "I don't think so" said Knob, "You DOUBLED UP on every hole. You owe $1280.00".

Nacs was in shock. He didn't realize that the bet on each hole was being doubled. After thinking for a second, he agreed that his debt was in fact $1280.00.

Knob said to his pal, Nacs: "Being the friend and the fair-minded guy that I am, here's what I am willing to do: you buy the dinner and beers tonight, and hand wash my car one day next week, and we'll call it square." Nacs, knowing that he had little bargaining power, agreed.

Nacs bought the dinner and beers that night and Knob took pictures of Nacs washing his car the following week. Those photos have been displayed many times since.

# 25. WELCOME TO THE CLUB

Sean was just a little guy. About five and a half feet tall and weighing in at about 145 pounds. But the little runt could really smack a golf ball. He could hit it as far as the best golfers who made the annual sojourn into Montana.

This was Sean's first trip to Montana with the guys. And the Polson Golf Course was his first round of golf.

The bus left Spokane at 7:30 that Friday morning on the second weekend in August---the trip was always held on the second weekend in August. As usual, there were several coolers full of beer and ice and lots of snacks just in case the boys got hungry.

The first stop was going to be the Polson Golf Course, some 200 miles East of Spokane. The boys settled in for a 4-hour trip. A Stook game soon took over the back of the bus. Although it was still early, a few of the boys got into the beer; Sean was one of them.

By the time the bus pulled up to the Polson Pro Shop and unloaded the boys, Sean was in great form. After checking in and getting his foursome assignment, Sean loaded his bag on the cart, sat in the passenger seat, and laid his head back to catch a few zzzzzzzzzzzzzzzs before his tee time. The cart was parked next to the practice range where all the boys were warming up. Within minutes Sean was sound asleep.

It just so happened that Piccy had a couple of rolls of medical tape in his golf bag. After all, Piccy was a pharmaceutical salesman. Out came the tape. And with the help of Horse, they began the process of taping Sean to the golf cart. Within minutes Sean was securely taped to his cart—he wasn't going anywhere. And he never woke up during the procedure.

When the guys were called to the first tee to start their rounds, little Sean was left sitting in his cart, sound asleep. The boys started without him.

At the end of the second hole, the three other members of Sean's group decided they better check on him. They quickly drove back to the practice range and there was Sean, now wide awake, but still very "secure" in his seat. He immediately began calling his friends all kinds of names, some of them very obscene. But he quickly got over it as his friends came to his rescue and finally "untaped" him. He then joined his group for his first Montana round of golf.

# 26. RULES ARE RULES

The guys were playing Buffalo Hills Golf Course one sunny Sunday afternoon. It was the last stop on one of their three-day trips to Montana. As usual, Root and Lefty were getting hammered by Freddy and the Knob in their annual "grudge match".

For the prior five years these four had played together on the final day of the trip. Going into the above Sunday match, Root and Lefty had won exactly zero of the previous five annual matches. As they got ready to tee off on the 18th hole at Buffalo Hills, it looked like it would be six straight years for Root and Lefty without a win. They were down $40.00 each.

Before teeing off on 18, Freddy said to the two opponents: "What do you two jackasses want to do"? Meaning---do you have the balls to make a bet being that you are getting trounced for the 6th year in a row.

Lefty spoke up: "We got you two pricks. Not only are we going to double you, but we also got you for another $50.00 on top of that". This meant that if Root and Lefty won the hole, they would get $50.00 each; if they lost the hole, they would each owe $130.00.

The 18th hole at Buffalo Hills is heavily lined with trees on the left side of the fairway. An access road, the Club House, and the practice putting green all stretch down the right side of the fairway, and all are out of bounds. Also, on the right side of the fairway, about 150 yards from the tee, the fairway drops down into a valley, and the green sits another 175 yards beyond. There is also a steep bank on the right side that channels tee shots down into the valley below. A good drive to the right side will cause the ball to channel perfectly down into the valley and will result in good access to the green with a second shot.

It is important to know that Root and Lefty both hit the ball a long ways. However, on more than one occasion, their tee shots have been known to wander a little. On many occasions over the years Root's drives have wandered off course and struck condos and houses lining the fairways of various golf courses. And on at least one occasion, Lefty sliced a drive that hit a car driving down the road next to a fairway.

It is also important to know that both Root and Lefty are good "listeners". In golf parlance that means that if their opponents make a suggestion to them to the effect that they probably won't hit a very good next shot, they tend to "listen".

Freddy and Knob both hit sweet drives right down the middle and over the hill, into the valley that sits just before the 18th green. Perfect position both.

Lefty also smacked his drive right down the middle. It seemed that the outcome of the match was now in Root's hands. Could he handle this kind of pressure? Would his nerves hold up?

Root seemed to take a little extra time teeing up his ball. He walked around the tee box looking tense and unsure. He walked over to the cart and took a big swig of Kokanee, hoping that the drink would somehow relax him. He took a big breath of Montana air and then yelled: "Just do it"!

He moved towards his ball, got his feet and arms settled in, and then just before he was ready to hit his tee shot, Freddy said: "Root---whatever you do, don't hit your drive to the right. There is nothing but trouble over there". Root responded by saying: "F--- you Freddy". Root then "smoked" his drive. His hardest hit of the day. The ball sailed high, the ball sailed long, and the ball sailed way right. It landed on the practice putting green.

Although the ball was out of bounds, Root did not know that the practice putting green was OB. He knew that he was not supposed to hit an iron shot off a green but with money on the line he was not going to worry too much about a little violation like that. He therefore drove over to the green to see what kind of shot he had.

While Root was trying to decide what club to hit for his approach into the 18th green, he noticed a man on the green giving a putting lesson to a 10-year-old boy. They were putting right in the path of where Root needed to hit his second shot. Root actually had a good view of the green from where his ball laid. And with $130.00 on the line, he had no intention of moving the ball off the putting surface before hitting his second shot.

After waiting for 3 or 4 minutes for the man and the boy to move, Root finally said: "Excuse me sir, but would you mind moving off to the side a little while I hit to the green"? The man walked over to Root and said: "If this is your drive, it is out of bounds. And it is not proper to ever hit an iron shot off a green. I am the golf course manager and although we welcome you here as our guest, we would ask that you obey the rules".

Root picked up his ball and walked off the practice putting green.

He and Lefty had now extended their losing streak to six straight years. They each paid $130.00.

# 27. CHECK YOUR BAGS, SIR?

The eight guys had just completed their round at the Avondale, Idaho, Golf Course and decided to stop by the Couer d'Alene Hotel and have a drink before heading back to Spokane. The Couer d'Alene Hotel is a high-class resort hotel sitting on the shores of Lake Coeur d'Alene, in Coeur d'Alene, Idaho, which is located about 35 miles east of Spokane.

The Hotel has a couple of nice lounges overlooking the lake. The lounges have nice, soft, cushy sofas for the customers, and are also adorned with nicely attired and pretty cocktail waitresses. So, it was a logical stop for the boys before heading into Spokane.

Spacko, the Italian restaurant and bar owner, was part of the golfing group that day. He, along with all the other guys, was dressed in golfing shorts and a golf shirt. The only difference with Spacko on this particular day, was that he was not wearing any underwear, which would become obvious as the afternoon wore on.

The guys made their way into the hotel lounge and quickly found a vacant section of soft sofas where they seated themselves in a semi-circle arrangement. The cocktail waitress came over and took the drink order.

Before the waitress returned with the drink order, some of the guys observed that Spacko's private baggage was hanging out from under his golf shorts and was actually resting on the sofa on which he was sitting. It was obvious that he was not wearing underwear. Spacko is quite a talker and, as was usual, he was in the middle of a story and certainly never realized that he was showing his "stuff".

This group of guys has been together for so many years that no one was about to mention to Spacko that he had a problem. Rather the guys couldn't wait for the waitress to return with their drink order so they could maneuver her into a position from where she was sure to see Spacko's "baggage". And that is exactly what happened. She clearly saw the "exhibit" but said nothing as she turned and walked away.

As the guys were getting towards the end of their first drink, they made sure to call over a different waitress to take their second order. Again, they maneuvered the lady into position so that she had a straight on view of the Italian Stallion.

This same procedure occurred with a third waitress.

Just before the guys were ready to leave for Spokane, they called over one of the waitresses and asked for their bill. Once again, she was in a great position to see the show. One of the guys thanked her for her service as he paid the tab. Another guy pointed to Spacko and said to the waitress: "This is Spacko, I think you might know him". The guys roared with laughter; the poor waitress turned redder than a beet; and finally, Spacko realized that he had been the "star of the show" for the prior hour.

# 28. SILKY SMOOTH

The majority of the guys who regularly made the annual trip into Montana, had been traveling together and hanging out for many years. Most of them were ex hockey players who had settled in Spokane after their hockey days were over. They all got great satisfaction if they could do something that would embarrass one of the guys. When they got away from home for those three days, the guys often called each other names, exchanged obscene language, wrestled with one another, and pulled every prank they could think of. There didn't seem to be many boundaries as to what they might do to one of their own. Of course, it was all in fun, but sometimes outsiders would have a tough time understanding.

And if one of the guys ever got into any type of "problem" on the trip, the whole crew would be there in a heartbeat to help out their buddy.

Every so often the trip would "lure in" an "outsider" who would think this is the type of trip he would like. And more times than not, those "first timers" never made a second trip.

One year Lenny made the trip. He was a local businessman and was well respected in the community. He was also a good golfer, carrying about a seven handicap.

The three-day trip required sleeping in a motel for two nights. It also meant having a roommate. And if you were on the trip for the first time, you would be rooming with a guy you had never roomed with before.

On Friday and Saturday evenings the boys would usually go to downtown Whitefish, or Kalispel, depending upon which city they were staying in, and would hit the bars, play Texas Hold Em, listen to some good ole country music, and just have a good time till the bars closed.

On this particular trip, Lenny got teamed up with Lunker as

his roommate. Lunker was a rough and tough former defenseman from Penticton, British Columbia. He had been on at least 15 prior Montana trips. He knew the ropes. He also liked to sleep in the raw and would often parade around his motel room naked.

Over the years his roommates paid little attention to Lunker's state of dress or undress. They really didn't give a shit just so long as Lunker stayed in his own bed, which he did most of the time.

This was "new territory" for Lenny. His standard bedtime attire was silk pajamas, both top and bottom. Lenny was shocked the first night when he saw Lunker wandering around in the raw. And Lunker was equally shocked when he saw his roommate dressed in silk PJs. Prior to this trip, nobody in the history of the Montans trip had ever been seen wearing pajamas.

Lenny slept with one eye open that night. And Lunker ridiculed Lenny something terrible for the entire weekend, and let everyone within ear shot know that his roomie wore silk PJs.

Lenny never made another Montana trip. The trip sort of has a way of sorting people out.

# 29. CAN YOU HOLD FOR A MINUTE PLEASE?

The crew had played its first round of golf of the three-day trip. It was followed by a long night in downtown Kalispel hitting all the joints, drinking a few beers, and just relaxing. At the end of the night the guys went out for some early morning breakfast just before heading back to the Motel for the night. It was 3:00 AM by the time the group got back to the Motel.

The 24-man crew was staying at the Motel 8 in Kalispel. Two guys to a room. The bus was scheduled to head out to the golf course at 10:00 the next morning.

Mac and Knob were rooming together. The Pates was rooming three doors down with another guy.

For some reason Pates did not hear what time the bus was scheduled to pull out the next morning. He therefore called the room where Mac and Knob were sleeping. The call was made at 7:00 AM and went something like this:

Mac: Hello" as he reached for the phone located on the little desk next to his bed.

Pates: "Is Knob there, it's the Pates"?

Mac: "Just a minute. Knob it's for you", as he laid the receiver on top of the little desk and put his head back on his pillow.

Knob was sound asleep and didn't hear Mac.

At 7:45 AM Mac got up to have a shower. He noticed that the receiver was still lying on top of the little desk next to his bed. Mac picked up the receiver.

Mac: "Hello".

Pates: "Is Knob there, it's the Pates"?

Forty-five minutes had passed since the call first came in. And Pates was still waiting for Knob to answer.

# 30. I NEED A DOUBLE

Blackrock Golf Course is an exclusive high end Golf Course located near Lake Coeur d'Alene. It is a private course and is open only to its members and their guests.

One spring, there had been a charity dinner-auction held in Spokane to raise funds for youth sports. A lot of the guys attended the annual affair. One of the items up for auction was a round of golf for three at Blackrock. The auction item was donated by John, a Blackrock member. The winning bidder and his two friends would be the guests of John for a round of golf to be followed by drinks and dinner at the fancy Blackrock Clubhouse.

The Judge was the winning bidder at a cost of an even $1000.00.

The Judge contacted John and set up the round of golf, drinks, and dinner, for a Saturday in July. The Judge generously invited two of his friends to fill out the foursome.

The trio of golfers travelled over to Blackrock and met up with John, their host for the day. The Judge had never met John before. The other two members of the foursome both knew John from prior encounters.

Being that the Judge was the one who had won the auction item, it seemed only proper that he and John share a cart together. And so, it was as the foursome teed off on number one at Blackrock.

The best golfer in the foursome was John, the host. He was about a 15 handicap. The Judge was about a 22 and the other two guys were also 20 plus handicaps.

It was a nice, sunny, July afternoon. Just a perfect day for golf. And John was a perfect host in all respects. He and the Judge seemed to get along well as cart partners.

The front nine was uneventful. There were a few "jabbing" comments here and there, but everyone was on good behavior, just as would be expected on an exclusive course.

On the back nine, there is a par five hole that winds around a small lake on the left side of the fairway. A perfect drive will position the golfer for a shot of about 100 yards across the lake, all carry. From there, it is a chip shot onto the green.

The Judge hit a perfect drive. His ball came to rest about 5 yards from the lake. All he would need now was a nine iron across the water. Piece of cake.

John (the host) had parked his cart about 15 yards from where the Judge's ball laid. The Judge took his nine iron and confidently, maybe even cockily, walked to his ball. On his first shot, the Judge toed it and the ball went about 40 yards into the water.

"That can happen to anybody" said the polite host trying to put the embarrassed Judge at ease.

The Judge walked back to the cart to get another ball. He returned to the water's edge and teed up ball number two. Again, he mishit the shot and again the ball was swallowed up by the lake.

"Come on Judge, we know you can do it", lied the Judge's opponent from 20 yards away.

Ball number three was "skulled" and went about 40 yards before diving into the lake. The host didn't say a word; he was getting a little uncomfortable and was hoping that his guest would soon find a solution to his quandary.

As the Judge walked back to his bag for another ball, his opponent yelled "Why don't you take three or four balls with you this time. It will sure save on the shoe leather". The Judge didn't respond. Nor did he take but one ball with him as he made his way back to the lake's edge.

Balls four, five, and six, were also hit into the water. And before each ball was hit the Judge's opponent would yell out "That's ball number four" or "that's ball number five" etc., just to remind the

Judge in case his counting was off.

And each time the Judge had to make the walk from the edge of the lake back to his cart to get new ammunition, it seemed like an eternity with all eyes focused on him.

The Judge's opponent and his cart partner were laughing hysterically. It was so much fun to watch the Judge under achieve. And even the gracious host had to turn his back to the action as he, too, started to chuckle.

As the Judge addressed his seventh ball, this one with a five iron, the host said: "Come on Judge, make this be the one".

Wishful thinking! Splash. Ball number seven now missing in action.

Balls eight and nine met the same fate and the laughter got louder.

Finally with ball number ten and an eight iron, the Judge succeeded. His trio of partners yelled and applauded. The Judge had done it!

When, at the end of the hole, his opponent asked the Judge: "What score do you want me to put down for you"? The Judge replied "Go f--- yourself". And the laughter started anew.

The remainder of the round was uneventful.

Over drinks in the Clubhouse, the topic of conversation was the water hole. The gracious host, trying to ebb the embarrassment that the Judge was feeling, said: "Judge, don't let it get to you. We have all had bad days".

The Judge just shook his head as he politely asked his host: "Would you mind if I ordered a double"?

Folks, this is a true story

# 31. SAWING LOGS

After a few of years of different guys rooming with the Judge on the Montana golf trip, they all seemed to have one common complaint: THE JUDGE SNORES! REALLY LOUD!

In fact, the snoring was so loud that the Judge's roommates were not able to sleep. They tried various remedies in an effort to get some sleep: turn up the TV as loud as it would go; turn the Judge onto his side or belly; have a couple of good shots of whiskey just before hitting the rack; and using ear plugs. One roommate even pushed cotton batten up the Judge's nose in hopes that it would stop the snoring. Another guy put his mattress out in the hallway and slept out there for the two nights that he was the Judge's roommate.

When a "rookie" would be on his first Montana trip, he would automatically be roomed with the Judge. The "rookie" was told that the Judge had a lot of really funny stories and was a most interesting fellow to room with. The rookie "would just love rooming with the Judge". It didn't take long for the rookies to realize what a "crock" that statement was.

It finally got to the point where no one would room with the Judge.

In later years a "single" room was reserved for the Judge with the Judge having to pay the extra cost for not sharing a room with a roommate. Because the Judge was a "regular" on all these trips, it cost him a lot of extra dough over the years.

The guys, not letting the issue drop, would often send copies of magazine advertisements to the Judge advertising nasal products and various other snoring contraptions. Fortunately, the Judge was blessed with a "thick skin" and accepted all the abuse in stride and regarded it as just being a trade-off that he had to accept in return for hanging out with such a swell group of friends.

Even today, after 20 plus years of making the Montana trip, the Judge continues to room by himself.

# 32. THE STORY WITH NO END

Several years ago, twelve of the Spokane guys headed to San Diego during the month of February, to see the sun and play golf for a few days. They were tired of the snow and cold they had endured during the several previous months.

The Judge was one of the guys that went on the San Diego trip.

The Judge has always liked to read books. It really didn't matter what the topic was---he just liked to read. Before the flight left Spokane, the Judge was browsing through the bookstore and saw a book that interested him. He bought the book.

While the guys waited at the gate to board their plane, the Judge already had his nose buried in his new book. And throughout the flight to San Diego the Judge continued to read his book.

The guys stayed five days in San Diego and played four rounds of golf.

One day after golf the guys were in the Judge's room having a drink. One of the guys saw the Judge's book sitting on the TV. He grabbed the book when the Judge was not watching and left the room, making his way back to his own room. He then took a sharp knife and carefully cut out the last page of each chapter of the book. When the project was finished it was impossible to notice that any pages had been removed. The book was then returned to the Judge's room and placed back on top of the TV without the Judge noticing.

On the return flight to Spokane, the Judge was again heavily engrossed in his book. He read several chapters during the three-hour return flight. And never once did he ever indicate that there was something missing from his book.

Each page that had been cut out of the book was carefully preserved and taken back to Spokane by the guy who had cut out the pages. After he returned to Spokane, the guy put one of the pages into each of about a dozen different envelopes, all addressed to the Judge. On the top left-hand corner of each envelope the guy wrote a phony return address with a phony woman's name. The guy then gave one envelope to each of several different people who he knew were going out of town, whether for work or vacation, and asked each one to drop the envelope in the mail when that person arrived at his destination.

The Judge lived in a large apartment complex in Spokane. Rollie, who also went on the San Diego trip, just happened to be the manager of the apartment building. One of Rollie's duties was to deliver the mail to the tenants in his building.

About a month after the San Diego trip, Rollie, as part of his apartment management duties, saw envelopes starting to arrive in the mail addressed to the Judge, all with different post mark locations on the envelopes. One day there was an envelope from Chicago, another day there was one from Dallas, on still another day there was one from Honolulu, and then on another day an envelope arrived from New York. This went on for about six weeks and each time that Rollie would deliver the envelopes to the Judge, Rollie would make a remark such as "you got friends in a lot of different places Judge". The Judge, not having a clue as to what was going on, would just nod his head.

After several weeks of receiving these unusual envelopes, the Judge still hadn't figured out that the last page of each chapter in his book was missing.

About four months later the boys were sitting around having a beer after completing a round of golf, when Rollie asked the Judge how he had enjoyed that book. The Judge responded by saying: "It was a good read". Rollie finally told the Judge what had happened. The Judge just shook his head and said: "You know I was thinking that something wasn't quite right when each chapter ended in mid-sentence. But then I thought that it must be the way the book was written".

Brilliant, Judge, just brilliant!! No wonder our judicial system is screwed up!

# 33. A MAKE OVER FOR THE KID

Two foursomes had just finished their golf match at the Harrington Golf Course, a nice little nine-hole course located about 40 miles west of Spokane. Rather than have a beer in the clubhouse, the group decided to head to Reardon, WA, a small town that was located much closer to Spokane.

In downtown Reardon, there are two bars, one is called the Red Rooster. It seemed like a perfect place to have a cold beer.

But there was one little problem---one of the guys in the group, Lunker, had brought his 15-year-old son, Jay, along on the short trip, and he had played golf with the group. The legal age for admittance to a bar in the State of Washington, is 21 years. Jay fell short of that by six years. What to do?

In Lunker's truck, he just happened to have a black felt tipped pen. Tim, a passenger in Lunker's truck and a guy well known for his artistic talents, grabbed the felt marker and said: "Jay, move over here while I solve the problem".

Jay slid over next to Tim and the artist went to work.

By the time Lunker's truck pulled into the Red Rooster parking lot, Jay had a black mustache, long black sideburns, and black chin whiskers. With a baseball cap pulled down over his eyes, he could have passed for 30!

Jay wasn't even asked to show his ID.

His mother was so proud when he told her the story. Lunker had forgot to tell his kid to keep quiet.

# 34. LONG DRIVE CONTEST

There were 10 guys in Gene's' motor home when it pulled out of Spokane. The destination was Vancouver, BC. If all went according to plan, there would be two or three rounds of golf, lots of Stook, maybe a day of salmon fishing, and an Indy 500 race in Vancouver. The group would be gone five days.

As the motor home neared the City of Ritzville, about 60 miles west of Spokane, there was a "thump, thump, thump" coming from the underside of the motor home. Gene pulled the rig over, off the main I-90 highway, to investigate. He soon found a left rear dually tire that was flatter than the Seattle Mariners.

The boys immediately complained that Gene should have checked his machine out before the start of the trip---that the guys were really being inconvenienced by Gene's lack of trip preparation. Gene was used to these types of remarks from this crowd and he knew there was only one appropriate response that would quiet these guys: "Go f--- yourselves"!

Now Gene was a mechanic by trade. He could fix anything! But this was not an ordinary sized passenger car. It was a large 50-foot motor home. He let the guys know that it was going to take some time to replace the tire.

This group of guys was not a patient group. And so, they decided that this would be a perfect time to have a "long-drive" contest.

The contest rules were quickly established. Each guy put $10.00 into the pot. Winner takes all. Each guy got three drives. The guy that hit his drive the farthest before it left the highway, would be the winner. Also, if any of a player's three balls hit a vehicle on the road, that person would be immediately disqualified. The guys would be the judges and their decision was final.

And so, the contest started. One after another the boys started smacking their drives down I-90. A few of the drives hit the middle of the road and seemed to bounce and roll into the next county. After the last guy had driven his balls, the winner of the $100.00 was Mac---a big burly man who manufactures burial vaults for a living.

# 35. "THE GENIUS"

I t was the first time the guys had traveled to Vancouver to golf. It was a trip filled with a lot of interesting and humorous events.

As soon as the motor home pulled out of Spokane, the guys started a "Stook" game. And it wasn't long before Lefty came up with a brilliant new rule: "From now on, every dealer needs to put 20% of his winnings from each pot, into a side pot to buy beer, snacks, and miscellaneous items". That meant that each time a new dealer dealt a round, if he won money during that round, and he usually did, he had to put 20% into the side pot.

It is important to note that the dealer has a tremendous advantage over the other players because the dealer takes ties, meaning, for example, that if the dealer and the player he is playing against, both have cards totaling seventeen, the dealer wins and takes the money that the player had bet.

Well, the City of Vancouver is about 400 miles northwest of Spokane. And with various pit stops along the way, the trip would take at least 10 hours.

A "round" of Stook meant that the dealer played against each player three times. The dealer put whatever amount of money he wanted into the pot to start a round. But once he placed money in the pot, he could neither add to it, nor take from it, until the entire round was completed. If a dealer put too little in the pot, there was a danger that a player could "bet the pot" and if he won, the dealer's round was over and the next guy in line took over the deal. If a dealer put too much in the pot, there was a danger he could lose the entire pot.

A complete round of Stook with ten guys playing, usually takes about 15 minutes to complete. So, in a one-hour time frame, the contributions to the side pot were usually substantial. And over ten hours the side pot would be huge.

It was not uncommon for the dealer to win three or four hundred dollars in one fifteen-minute round. And 20% of $400.00 is $80.00.

By the time the motor home got to Seattle very few of the players had any money left because all their money had been diverted to Lefty's "side" pot. Once the money was placed in the side pot, it was "gone". And so, when the motor home pulled into Seattle, the first stop was an ATM machine so the guys could replenish their funds.

The travel time between Seattle and Vancouver, in a motor home, is about three hours. With the 20% rule still in effect, all the guys were nearly broke for A SECOND TIME in the same day, by the time the bus pulled into Vancouver. But there was well over $3000.00 in the "side pot".

Lefty hadn't realized that the 20% rule would eventually result in all the players going broke.

Although the guys had a fun time spending the "side pot" money, even after the passage of 20 years, they have never let "The Genius" forget his 20% rule.

# 36. THE PRIEST AND THE PEACOCK

Several years ago, four of the guys played a late Saturday morning round of golf at Esmeralda Golf Course in Spokane. It was a warm July day. The group finished their round of golf by about 3:00 PM and headed to the Viking Tavern for a cold beer. They all rode in one car being driven by Ken, a food salesman for Kraft Foods.

During their stay at the Viking, the Duck, a Spokane businessman who got his name because his feet point out to the side when he walks, started drinking Thunderbird wine. He had several glasses of the cheap wine and certainly was feeling it's effects when the group left the tavern a couple of hours later.

The Duck was a staunch Roman Catholic. And it just so happened that his wife had invited a Roman Catholic Priest to the house for a Saturday evening dinner with the Duck's family. The Duck, having got caught up in some "good wine", forgot that the Priest was coming to the house for dinner.

After leaving the tavern, Ken drove the Duck to his house on the south side of Spokane. Ken opened the trunk and lifted the Duck's clubs and pull cart out of the trunk and opened up the cart so the Duck could pull his clubs up to the front of his house. While he was doing that, the Duck spotted a large and extremely colorful cardboard "Peacock" advertising sign laying in the trunk. It showed a peacock in all its splendor with its feathers fully spread. It was an advertisement sign for some of the food products that Ken sold and he would set these signs up in his customers' grocery stores. The Duck was immediately attracted to that sign and decided that it would look fantastic riding on top of his pull cart. And that is exactly where the Duck placed that colorful cardboard sign---on top of his cart.

The Duck, with his golf hat on sideways, and wobbling with

every step he took, started for the front porch of his house, pulling his decorated golf cart behind him. As he approached the front porch, out came his wife and the Priest to greet him. The Duck's wife immediately recognized that the Duck had made one stop too many and was in no condition to entertain the Priest. She lit into the Duck with both barrels ablasting.

The Duck had no exit strategy. He was in big time trouble. There was nowhere to hide. And he still had a couple of hours to spend with his "guest" during which time he could try to explain the "Peacock" and might even need some "confession" time.

And the Duck's three playing partners, thinking the situation was very comical indeed, and knowing that there was really nothing they could do to help their friend, jumped into Ken's car and left the scene in a hurry leaving their pal to fend for himself.

# 37. BILLY THE GOAT

Knob is a Spokane attorney. One morning his intercom line rang in his office. It was the front receptionist. "There are a couple of gentlemen out here to see you. They say it's important".

"I'll be right out" replied Knob.

When Knob arrived at the front reception area, he found two men and a full-sized goat standing in the lobby. Knob was friends with the two guys but this was the first time he had met the goat.

One of the guys said: "This is our friend Billy".

Knob immediately knew he was in trouble. Only a guy with a great imagination would name his goat "Billy".

"Jim and I, and our friend "Billy", are here on behalf of the Boys and Girls Club of Spokane. In the five minutes we have been here, it appears that Billy has taken a real liking to your offices and he is settling in quite nicely. We can leave him here with you for the rest of the day, so you and Billy can get to know each other a little better, or, if you would agree to make a nice contribution to the Boys and Girls Club, we would be happy to drop him off at a location of your choosing".

By this time the entire office was in the reception area watching the "extortion" play out and having a great laugh at Knob's expense.

Knob went back to his office, wrote a check to the Boys and Girls Club for $300.00, returned to the reception area, and paid the ransom.

"The Boys and Girls Club thanks you for the donation. Do you have another location where you wish to have "Billy" dropped off"?

"Let me make a quick call" replied Knob.

A call was made to the bailiff of a Judge at the courthouse. The Judge was a good friend of Knob's.

"Tom, (bailiff), this is Knob. Is the Judge on the bench this morning"?

Tom: "Yes, he will be on the bench for another hour or so. Then he is cutting out for the afternoon because he has a 1:30 tee time at the Country Club. Can I help you with something"?

Knob then explained the goat situation to the bailiff and requested his help in secretly getting "Billy" into the Judge's chambers while the Judge was still on the bench. The Bailiff thought the Judge would love a little company when he got off the bench and walked into his chambers.

The arrangements were made. They would need to hurry but the relocation process could be easily accomplished before the Judge left the bench.

"Billy" was taken to the courthouse. The Bailiff was "on the lookout" and as soon as he saw the group arrive, he led them into the Judge's chambers. "Billy" was unleashed and the group went into hiding in a room not far from the Judge's chambers. "Billy" was all alone in the chambers for several minutes until the Judge left the bench and made his way into his chambers.

When the Judge got into his chambers, he let out a yell, using words that were not fit for a Judge. Tom the Bailiff came running into the chambers. "What is it Your Honor"?

"Where did this damn goat come from? He has shit all over my chambers".

It was at this point that Tom called in the goat sitters. They all had a good laugh while Tom cleaned up the "mess". The Judge, being a good sport as always, wrote out a check to the Boys and Girls Club of Spokane, and gladly gave the guys the name and address of the next recipient. He also had an interesting story to tell his golf mates later in the day.

## 38. EASY MONEY

It was another trip to Montana. The Montana whether is always fantastic during the second weekend of August.

Shaun was a first-year guy on the trip. He was a 4-handicap golfer and could smack the ball a country mile. There weren't many guys that could match him in a head-to-head match.

But on the "side" games he still had "some learnin" to do.

During the second day of the trip, Shaun was in a foursome that included Frankie, who was the shortest hitter on the bus. But he was not against making a bet or two "if the odds were right".

Shaun had never played a prior round of golf with Frankie but after playing half a dozen holes with him that day, it was obvious to Shaun that Frankie was a poor golfer and "couldn't carry Shaun's lunch bucket".

So, on the seventh hole, a straight away par four, Shaun was a little surprised when Frankie said: "I'll long drive ya for $10.00".

With no hesitation Shaun said: "You're on".

Sean teed off first and hit a beautiful drive right down the middle, about 275 yards out. He smiled at Frankie but didn't say a word.

Frankie got up and hit his best drive of the day, splitting the fairway, with his ball coming to rest about 175 yards out, but 100 yards behind Shaun's drive.

Shaun held out his hand: "Easiest $10.00 I have ever made".

Frankie replied: "I said I would long drive you. I didn't say I would win. Where's my $10.00".

Shaun's mouth dropped open as he recounted the words of the bet. He then reached into his pocket, pulled out a $10.00 bill and handed it to Frankie, saying: "That's bullshit you bastard".

Frankie just smiled, shook his head, and said: "Rookies".

# 39. INITIATION TIME

The Montana Golf Trip is much similar to other sports from the standpoint of "initiation rites".

Over the years, there have been several "rookies" who have joined the group on the three-day trip into Montana. And without exception, there has always been "a little something" to welcome them to the club.

A few years back Brandon and Tuna made their first trips to Montana. Brandon is a big man standing close to six feet tall and weighing in at close to 250 big ones. Tuna, an ex-football lineman, stands 6 foot 4 inches tall and weighs about 260 pounds.

A few days before the bus pulled out that year, and having heard that Brandon and Tuna would be making their first trips to Montana, Jackman and Tim paid a visit to "Value Village" in the heart of Spokane. Value Village is a huge used clothing store that sells every style and size of clothing imaginable. And the prices are cheap.

Jackman and Tim never had a shopping list as such when they entered the store but they both have imaginative minds and it was a certainty that the two would find something "suitable" for the two large newcomers.

The group played its first round of golf at the Esmeralda Municipal Golf Course. The bus left immediately after that round was completed and headed towards Whitefish, Montana.

It was another hot August day and the boys, having just spent five hours in the sun, were thirsty and the beers were going down nicely. The Stook game was going full bore and everyone was in a great mood.

"Could I have your attention please"? asked Tim over the bus loudspeaker. "I am honored to announce that we are fortunate enough to have two rookies on board today. Let's hear it for Brandon and Tuna".

Applause. Yelling. What a welcome for these two fine gentlemen.

"Could I ask you both to please step to the front of the bus? We have a gift for each of you".

The two rookies made their way up to the front of the bus where they were met by Jackman and Tim. Jackman pulled two huge full-length dresses from the shopping bag. One dress was a bright orange with colored flowers mixed in everywhere. It was very pretty. The other was a pink, low cut dress with white piping along the borders of the dress. It too was very fashionable.

"Boys, who do you think should wear the orange dress and who do you think should wear the pink dress"? asked Tim to the rest of the guys on board the bus. The guys quickly determined that Brandon should wear the orange dress and that Tuna, the ex-football player, would look best in pink.

And so it was that the two large gentlemen donned what would be their mandatory attire for the rest of that day and night, and into the wee hours of the following morning.

Friday is always the first night that the guys spend in Montana. And as soon as they get to Whitefish and get checked into their hotel, they are off to main street to drink some more beer, whiskey, or whatever else they can get their hands on. This Friday night was no exception.

Brandon and Tuna turned a few heads as they meandered from bar to bar checking out the town. They were by far the two biggest dress wearers in Whitefish that night. In fact, in a town that is known for its cowgirls, tight jeans, and western boots, the two were the only people wearing dresses that night.

And when total strangers learned that these two huge fellows were part of an initiation process, they immediately befriended the two and were only too happy to buy them drinks and do "shots" with the pair. They both got their fill of Montana alcohol that night and never paid a nickel for any of it.

This was just one of the initiations that took place for the rookies that decided to make the three-day sojourn into Montana.

# 40. THE JUDICIAL SYSTEM

Every corporation, business, government, and group, has a system of laws and regulations to ensure that there is harmony within that group or entity. The Montana Golf Group is no exception. "Order" and "tranquility" has to be maintained at all times.

And so, over the years, a very effective "Judicial System" has been created for the Montana trip, a system that stresses fairness and discipline and ensures that the rights of all participants will always be respected and protected. When the guys return to Spokane after three days of fellow-shipping with their brethren, it is important for them to go to their respective homes knowing that they have been treated fairly and justly.

And thus came into being "The Kangaroo Court".

The Judge for the Kangaroo Court has a lifetime appointment. He was unanimously selected by his peers---his fellow golfing buddies. His identity is kept secret. He was selected because of his wisdom and unequaled sense of fairness and justice. When this Judge renders justice, the guys have no doubt that the correct decision has been made.

It is a tradition that following the group's third round of golf which ends early Sunday afternoon, the bus takes the guys to Moose's Saloon, located on Main Street in downtown Kalispel. The guys order about twenty pizzas and several ice-cold pitchers of beer. After a couple of hours of eating, drinking, telling stories, and laughing, the guys re-board the bus and head towards the Talking Bird Saloon, located about 100 miles down the road in St. Regis, Montana.

It is about a two-hour bus trip from Kalispel to St. Regis. It is during this two-hour time frame that the honorable Judge convenes his Kangaroo Court. Fines can, and usually are, levied during this session. Fines are only levied if a particular golfer has misbehaved during the trip. Fines can range from a low of $5.00 to a high of $400.00, for "extreme misconduct". A fellow by the name of Coxie presently holds the record for the largest fine received.

Some of the golfers, believing that they may have committed some acts of misconduct during the trip, but not knowing whether the Judge has been made aware of the misconduct, and not wanting to "chance" receiving a heavy fine, have been known to approach His Honor before the Court goes into session, make a full "confession", and offer a monetary payment to His Honor in hopes of avoiding a stiffer fine. Sometimes the Judge accepts such offers and sometimes he doesn't.

All fine money goes into a "beer pot" and is spent at the Talking Bird Saloon. The amount of "beer pot" money collected in an average year is usually between $500 and $700, depending upon the three-day conduct of the golfers and the thirst of the players.

Bottom line is that the more acts of misconduct that the guys were guilty of during the three days, the more the total fines will be. The greater the amount of fine money collected, the greater the number of drinks that can be purchased at the Talking Bird. And the greater the number of drinks purchased at the Talking Bird, the longer the guys stay at the Saloon, and so on. If there happens to be any money left over after the saloon tab has been paid, the money is donated to charity. The greatest dollar amount of fines which has been collected on any one trip was $950.00 and the least amounted collected exceeded $500.00.

Fines can be levied for any reason, so long as that reason is "fair and Just". Being late for the bus; declaring a handicap that is higher than what the guys think the true handicap is; winning too much money on the team or individual golf games; dressing in an inappropriate style that is detrimental to the reputation of the group; complaining or bitching too much; drinking "fancy" wine; are just some examples of fineable offenses.

The group also has an appeal process if the fined person thinks the fine was unjust. He can pay an appeal fee of $25.00. He can then present his appeal immediately to the Judge who just levied the fine. In 28 years, there have been five appeals. The Judge's decisions have never been overturned; it just goes to show how fair and just the Judge's decisions have been.

The appeal money goes into the "beer pot" along with the fine money. Some whining goes on after the appellate process has run its three-minute course and the original decision has been upheld, but the fined golfer eventually settles down and rarely appeals any future decision of the honorable Judge on future bus trips. Needless to say, it is a very effective Court.

The Talking Bird Saloon has always been a stop off point for the group both going to, and returning from, the Whitefish/Kalispel area. The Talking Bird is a great saloon which offers drinks at excellent prices. In fact, there have been many times that the group has been able to negotiate $1.50 drinks, but based upon one condition imposed by the Talking Bird: the group must buy at least 100 drinks at a time.

Management of the Talking Bird has become well acquainted with the group over the years, and now looks forward to seeing the guys every year during the second weekend in August.

# 41. WHO MOVED THE SWITCH?

A few years ago, when the group arrived at the Eagles Ice Arena at 7:00 AM to board the bus for another Montana Golf Trip, they were greeted by a brand spanking new bus. The bus company thought that after 25 or so years of making this partying crew ride the worst bus in the fleet, it was about time to say "thank you" for all those years of business.

The boys soon had the bus loaded with beer, snacks, and golf clubs, and the trip was underway.

The first round of golf would be at the Couer d'Alene Municipal Course, a nice tree lined golf course just off the main highway. It was a good place to start the trip because the forecast was for temperatures in the mid-nineties and the trees would provide a little shade. But it promised to be a hot day.

The first group teed off at 9:45 AM. There were six foursomes on the trip.

It was a rather uneventful round of golf. There was the usual bitching among the guys but the beer kept them relaxed, and for the most part, in good humor. After all, they had three good days of fellowship ahead of them—what wasn't there to like?

After finishing the round of golf and paying off their golf debts in the clubhouse over a couple of beers, the group boarded the bus. The outside temperature had hit 98 degrees. The new air-conditioned bus would feel really good.

The boys settled in. The usual Stook game was soon underway and had 10 or 12 players. The rest of the guys just sat back and relaxed over an ice-cold Kokanee. Next stop was The Talking Bird Saloon in St. Regis, Montana, about two hours east.

Before the bus had got out of the Coeur d 'Alene city limits it started: "Bussie, turn on the AC. It is hotter than panther piss back here".

Kenny, who had driven for this group for many years, and had realized early on not to take s--- from the guys, replied: "The bus has been sitting in the sun for five hours. Give it a few minutes".

The bus found the on-ramp and headed down the highway towards St. Regis. Ten miles down the road it started again, only louder and with more voices: "Kenny, turn up the f------ air conditioner. It's 100 degrees back here".

Kenny: "Relax. The bus has been sitting in the sun. It takes a little time for the AC to get up and running".

The boys were quiet, for the time being.

The bus continued on down the highway. Another 15 miles had passed and still the bus had not cooled down. The boys were now getting pissed.

Craig, the owner and operator of an automobile body repair shop in Spokane, and a guy who knows everything there is to know about things mechanical, was on the bus and it was suggested that he go up front and see if he could determine why there was no cool air flowing through the brand-new bus.

Craig checked out the instrument panel for a few minutes and returned to the back of the bus.

"Don't see any obvious problem. But would like to get under the hood and take a peek. But that's a little tough to do at 70 MPH. Could be a hose or something simple. But being a new bus, it's all computerized, so it might be computer related. Next time he stops, I will take a look".

The bus remained hotter than hell; the complaints never let up; and Kenny continued to defend the bus, saying that it had been sitting in the sun for five hours on an exceptionally hot day and it would eventually cool down.

This went on for two hours, all the way to St. Regis, where the boys had never been so happy to see The Talking Bird Saloon.

When Kenny pulled the bus into a shady spot across from the Saloon, a couple of trip organizers took him aside and said: "Kenny. We know it's not your fault. But we have paid $3000.00 to rent this bus for three days. The rental fee includes air conditioning. Right now, this bus doesn't have any air conditioning. You get on the phone to your headquarters and tell them to immediately send a mechanic out to fix the AC, or send a replacement bus out. We are not leaving here without air conditioning, whether it is on this brand-new piece of shit bus, or on a replacement bus".

By this time even Kenny was starting to doubt his theory that "the bus had been sitting in the sun for five hours. It will cool down soon". He knew there was a problem.

Kenny called the bus headquarters and asked to speak with the head mechanic. Kenny explained the problem to the mechanic. The mechanic reminded Kenny that the new buses have different switch locations for some of the typical dashboard items. He said the switch for the air conditioning had been moved to the left side of the dash from the usual right side on the new buses. "Were you aware of that Ken?" Kenny replied that he was not aware of that change.

Kenny looked at the dashboard on the left side, and sure enough, there was the AC switch. He flipped it on, and cool air immediately started flowing through the bus.

An hour and a half later, the boys returned to the bus from The Talking Bird Saloon. The bus was nice and cool inside. They all asked Kenny what the problem had been. Kenny tried to blame it on the relocation of the AC switch. The boys weren't letting him off that easy. "We have a Kangaroo Court to handle things like this" they told Kenny. There could be fines.

On the return trip to Spokane that Sunday, the Court was called into session. The first case on the docket was Kenny the bus driver. He presented his case, trying to blame the newness of the bus as the reason for torturing the boys for two hours with no air conditioning. The Judge, in all his wisdom, wasn't buying what Kenny was selling.

"That will be a $25.00 fine, payable now" said the learned Judge.

Kenny pulled the bus over to the side of the highway, halfway between Polson and St. Regis, removed $25.00 from his wallet, and paid the fine. He knew he had screwed up.

The money went to the "Beer pot". And The Talking Bird Saloon was just a few miles down the road. The extra money would come in handy.

Once again, Justice had been served.

# 42. TIME FOR A SWIM

The guys had just returned to their Kalispel motel after finishing their round of golf that had started late Saturday morning.

It had been an exceptionally hot day. The Big Mountain Golf Course is a wide-open course with very few trees, especially on the front nine. For four and a half hours the guys had been baked by the sun, and had nowhere to hide. They decided to return to the Motel, take a dip to cool off, then sit around the pool and have a few beers. Later they would shower up and head to downtown Kalispel for the evening.

A trip newcomer, Buzz, had decided to join the boys on the three-day outing. This was Buzz's first Montana trip. And so far, he had gone about a day without getting any "special" treatment from the group.

It was about 5:00 PM on that Saturday afternoon. Most of the guys had been relaxing around the pool, over a beer or two, for the better part of two hours. Buzz had decided that rather than join the guys around the pool, he "would make a few calls". So, for the past two hours Buzz had been invisible. We think he was napping.

When Buzz re-appeared, he was walking down the grassy area next to the pool, towards the guys. It was obvious that he had already showered and got himself prettied up. He was wearing a pair of dress slacks and a tailored short sleeved shirt. His wing tips were recently polished and were quite shiny. And this was Montana on a Saturday night. Obviously, Buzz had never "done" a Montana Saturday night before.

As he approached the guys sitting at the end of the pool, they all looked at each other. They could not believe what was walking towards them. Without saying a word, every one of the guys had the same thing in mind. In unison, they all got to their feet, grabbed Buzz, and threw him into the pool.

When he finally pulled himself out of the pool, Buzz looked like a wet puppy. And he was whimpering a little bit. "Why did I deserve such treatment"?

Welcome to Montana, Buzz.

He never made another trip.

# 43. THANKS FOR THE DRINKS

t was mid-February. And it was Phoenix, Arizona. Twelve guys from Spokane had decided to get out of the snow and cold for a few days. Golfing in Phoenix seemed to be the answer.

Two hours earlier, the guys had completed a round of golf at a great golf course not far from Tempe, where they were staying. After showering up, the guys all met in the lobby of their hotel and decided to walk down the main drag located in close proximity to Arizona State University. The guys found a lively little bar and decided to stop for a drink.

Two hours passed in a hurry. The bar had a great atmosphere and the boys were very relaxed. The crew had gone through several snack trays and a few drinks.

A couple of the guys suggested that the group leave and go down the road to another location. Everyone was in agreement. Everyone but Lunker. He was busy talking with some new found friends and had his back turned to his golfing buddies.

It was quickly decided that the rest of the group would start leaving in pairs, or one by one, whenever Lunker's attention was diverted for any reason. The idea was for the entire group to sneak out without Lunker realizing that he was the only guy remaining.

Lunker has owned bars and restaurants for much of his life. Therefore, when he goes to a new city, he will oftentimes get into deep conversations with restaurant or bar owners, bar tenders, or anyone else who wants to talk about bars and restaurants. It is not uncommon for Lunker to spend 30 minutes talking to a stranger about these topics, and therefore he is the perfect guy to stick with the bill at the end of the night.

On this particular night, that is exactly what happened. Lunker got heavily engrossed in conversation with a guy seated at the next table. One by one and two by two, the rest of the group all filed out of the bar without Lunker realizing what was happening.

When Lunker finally realized that all his buddies had deserted him, he stood up and got ready to leave. It was at this time that the cocktail waitress presented him with the bill. It was for $450.00. Lunker almost s---.

"Didn't the guys pay any part of this"? he asked.

"No" replied the cocktail waitress.

"Well, I'm not paying this. I paid for my drinks as I ordered them. This is not my responsibility".

"Why don't I get the manager over here" replied the waitress. And she did.

After the manager and Lunker had a heated discussion, Lunker finally pulled a credit card out of his pocket and paid the bill. But he was pissed.

It is important to know that Lunker had never been in this area of the city prior to this particular evening. Although he had walked the several blocks from the hotel to get to the bar, Lunker really had not paid attention to the route he had walked from the hotel to the bar. Nor did Lunker recall the name of the hotel the group was staying at.

So, there he was. Standing by himself, outside of an unfamiliar bar, in a foreign city, with no idea of how to get back to his hotel, and with no recollection of what the name of his hotel was. And to add to his woes, he had just been stuck with a $450.00 bar tab by his good friends, all of whom had now disappeared. Life couldn't get much worse than that!

So, what did Lunker do? He hailed a cab. When he got in, he immediately told the story to the cab driver. The cabbie was not sure whether this inebriated individual was for real. How could 11 friends "sneak" out of a bar without the last guy knowing?

When told that the hotel had several floors and was within a mile or so of the bar where the cabbie had picked up Lunker, the cabbie had a pretty good idea of which hotel it was. He therefore drove to the Marriot Hotel and asked: "Does this look like the one"? "Yup, that's the one" replied a relieved Lunker.

A couple of more hours went by before the rest of the crew made it back to the hotel. And when Lunker heard them in the hallway he went out to meet them. He ranted and raved obscenely for several minutes questioning their friendship and wondering how "good friends could ever do such a thing".

When he was done, one of the guys gave him $450.00 that the guys had chipped in to handle the bar tab.

Only then did the guys get a smile out of the Lunker.

SIDE NOTE: The guys were actually sitting in a sidewalk beer garden a block from the bar, waiting for Lunker to walk past. Little did they know that Lunker could not remember the name of the hotel or how to get back to the hotel. The guys decided that from that date forward, someone would need to stay will Lunker at all times.

# 44. LOST AGAIN

Four of us had gone to Seattle to play a round of golf, spend an evening at the ponies, and watch the Mariners take on the Yankees. It was mid-July.

We were staying at the "W" Hotel, a very nice Hotel in the middle of downtown Seattle.

It was a quick and jam packed 48-hour trip.

We were scheduled to leave Seattle and head back to Spokane on Sunday morning.

On Saturday night, after the horse races, the four of us had a nice dinner at a restaurant located just walking distance from our hotel. As we walked back to the hotel, we happened to pass a Starbuck's coffee house located about two blocks from the hotel. One of the guys pointed it out and suggested that the four of us meet at Starbuck's the next morning at 9:00 AM for coffee. We would then return to the hotel, pack our bags, and start the drive back to Spokane. All were in agreement.

The next morning three of the four guys arrived at Starbuck's at the agreed upon time of 9:00 AM. But there was no sign of Lunker, who happened to be Root's roommate.

"Where is Lunker"? one of the other guys asked.

"He was just getting out of the shower when I left" said Root. "I reminded him to take a right turn as soon as he got out of the Hotel lobby, and always keep the water (Puget Sound) on his left side. Walk straight ahead for two blocks and you will run into Starbuck's". He said he understood.

By 10:00 AM Lunker had still not arrived at Starbuck's. So, the three guys left Starbuck's and headed back to the hotel. They looked all over for him as they walked back to the hotel, but still no Lunker. When they arrived at the front of the hotel, they looked down towards the water and there was Lunker, about four blocks down the hill and walking towards the water. One of the guys ran after him, turned him around, and brought him back to the hotel.

"Where were you going"? asked one of the guys.

"I thought you said walk towards the water" was Lunker's response.

Lost in Phoenix in February and Seattle in July. Twice in five months. Maybe a leash will help.

# 45. NO CHARGE FOR THE COCKROACHES

A four- or five-day trip to Phoenix in February or March has been a regular golf stop for the past several years for about twelve of the guys. The guys had stayed in four or five different areas of the city over the years but had not really found a location to their liking. So one year they asked Root to find a new place for the crew to stay during the upcoming trip.

Root travels a fair amount on business and actually goes to the Phoenix area several times a year. He said he would gladly find a place to stay and suggested that he seek out a place near Arizona State University where he knew there were lots of good restaurants and bars. Sounded like a good plan.

A couple of months later Root reported that he had located a nice little "high-end" motel within walking distance of the ASU area. And the prices were very reasonable. Although he had not checked the rooms out in person, he was confident that he had a winner and the boys would be very happy. The motel also had a swimming pool and an outdoor barbeque area if the guys decided to cook up some steaks. And to top it off, there was free parking right outside the doors.

Root was very proud not only that he had been assigned such an important duty, but also because he had found a motel that was sure to please.

In February twelve golfers from Spokane arrived at the Phoenix airport and immediately headed to the motel in Tempe to get checked in. When they arrived at the Motel, they discovered a two-story structure with about 26 total rooms, thirteen up and thirteen on the ground floor next to the paved parking lot. There was only one other vehicle in the parking lot.

As the boys entered the Motel office which was located right next to a very busy arterial, they were greeted by Francois, a very

137

friendly man with a pronounced accent. He had been waiting for the group to arrive as it became very evident that our group would be his only paying customers for the next few days. The group would take a total of six rooms, four on the ground floor and two on the upper floor. And because there would be two guys to a room, each guy would get his own individual bar of soap. The soap bars that Francois handed to the guys were about 2 ½ inches long by about 1 ½ inches wide. But Francois wasn't done just yet. He then handed each of the guys one towel and one washcloth and said: "Make sure you hang your towels up after using them. They will need to last you for the four days you are here".

The boys took their allotment of goodies and headed to their respective rooms. Inside the rooms were two double beds. There were several cracks in the walls and in some places, it was obvious that there had been recent sheet rock work done that had been taped but not yet painted. A quick inspection of the bathrooms indicated that there were several tile pieces missing and the shower doors would not fully close.

Over the next four days and three nights, the boys discovered that they had some unexpected company sharing their rooms---cockroaches---lots of them.

And the swimming pool that Root so proudly touted---it was about 24 feet long by 12 feet wide and had about 18 inches of water in it. But it did have a nice diving board.

And the outdoor barbeque that Root sold the boys on, Francois said it had been recently stolen.

The boys did not really spend much time in their rooms on this trip and so the lack of quality rooms was not really a big deal.

But the Root never heard the end of his "high-end motel".

# 46. CAN'T TRUST ANYBODY

I t was a Phoenix trip in February. There were twelve guys on the trip. Four rounds of golf in five days. The guys were up to their old habits of trying to screw their buddies any way they could. Anybody and anything was fair game.

The boys had just finished their second round of golf. It was still early in the day, about 4:00 PM. The weather was gorgeous. The guys were relaxing around the pool having a cold beer. It just so happened that Lunker's room was located closest to the pool. One of the guys, Coxie, said to Lunker: "Lunker, do you have a pen in your room?" "Yes, there is one on the night stand next to the bed. Here is my key if you want to get it." Coxie took the key, went to the room and returned a few minutes later, giving the key back to Lunker.

Shortly after Coxie returned, the guys decided to walk down the street to one of the many bars that were in the area. They never returned to the hotel until well after midnight.

Lunker pulled back his bedspread and found his sheets were tied in knots. He finally got his bed straightened out and climbed in hoping for a good night's sleep. When he laid his head on his pillow, it didn't feel quite right. He turned the lights back on and looked inside his pillow cases. They were filled with small rock pebbles. He took the pillow cases outside, dumped out the pebbles, and returned to his bed. He quickly fell asleep without further problems.

Golf was scheduled for 10:00 AM the next day. Lunker showered, got dressed, and headed out the door with his golf hat and a box of new Titleists. All three cars pulled away from the hotel and headed towards the golf course. At the course, the cars pulled up to the "bag drop" area, the guys got out, unloaded their bags and shoes, and waited for the Pro Shop to deliver their carts.

Lunker began putting his golf shoes on and felt something funny. He pulled his shoes off, looked inside, and found the front half of each shoe filled with shaving cream. He took the shoes inside to the bathroom and cleaned the shoes out as best he could. He then returned to his golf cart and put on his golf hat. The hat had Vaseline spread all around on the inside band of the hat. Lunker had to go back inside the clubhouse to the bathroom, where he tried to wipe the Vaseline from the hat band. He wasn't successful in cleaning the hat and had to buy a replacement in the Pro Shop.

When he finally got ready to tee off, he pulled out his sleeve of Titleists, opened it up, and found three badly beaten range balls.

There was a lot of laughter from the guys and the round of golf hadn't yet started.

After all the years of hanging out with these guys, Lunker should have known better than to give his room key to "a friend".

# 47. ONE DAY OF FAME

They guys had teed off at 7:00 AM that day at a golf course in Vancouver. There were three foursomes. An early tee time was needed because the group was going to attend the Indy 500 style car race in the afternoon. A lot of the big names were racing that day.

The group spent some time going through the pits and getting a firsthand glimpse of the race cars. They then watched the race and afterwards went back to the infield area.

"Lefty" was one of the guys on this trip. He had black hair, was about 30 years of age, and was about 5 feet 9 inches tall. He had a slight resemblance to Michael Andretti who just happened to be racing that day.

After the race was over, the group headed back to the infield area. A couple of the guys in the group thought it would be interesting if they crowded around "Lefty", started calling him "Michael", made a loud commotion to attract attention to the group, and loudly began asking "Michael" for his autograph.

Fans soon started crowding around "Michael", asking for his autograph and asking that he pose for photos. One of the guys acted like he was a manager for "Michael" and asked the crowd to be patient and Michael would try to meet all their requests. Within minutes the crowd was at least ten deep around "Michael", all wanting an autograph or a photo. After 15 minutes of signing phony autographs and posing for photos, it became evident that this was not a good idea. The crowd was getting too big. Not one person ever suggested that "Lefty" was not "Michael". It was time to get out of there.

The guy who was acting as "Michael's" manager, stepped in and said: "I am sorry folks, but Michael has a banquet appointment in 30 minutes and he has to leave now. He thanks all of you for your support".

With that being said, "Michael's" golfing buddies grabbed him by the arm and they made their getaway.

# 48. A FISH STORY

After a second day of golf in Vancouver, the guys decided they would go down to the waterfront and hire a charter boat for an afternoon of fishing.

There were twelve golfers. Therefore, there would be four teams of three guys each. Each guy would throw $20.00 into the pot. A total of $240.00. The fishing wouldn't be any fun unless there were some side bets. The team that caught the first fish of the day would get $100.00. The team that caught the biggest fish of the day, meaning "heaviest" fish, would collect $140.00. Simple rules.

After four hours of fishing, there were a total of 8 fish caught by the 4 groups. Group one caught the first fish of the day and received $100.00.

There were two other fish that were in the running for the "biggest" fish of the day. The fish would be weighed on the scales when the boat docked.

Lunker's team was pretty confident, almost cocky, that its fish, measuring about 28 inches in length, was the easy winner in the "biggest" fish of the day category. But Freddy's team wasn't ready to concede anything. It's fish, although only 18 inches long, might have a shot at the title.

When the boat docked, the fish were taken to the scales. An old fisherman was standing near the scales, cleaning his daily catch. He was asked to be the "neutral" judge and weigh the two fish that were in the running for "biggest" fish of the day. He first weighed Lunker's fish---it weighed in at four pounds and five ounces. The old fisherman said: "I think this is the winner". He didn't think there was any sense weighing Freddy's fish, but he did so anyway just to make it official. When he dropped it on the scale, it weighed in at five pounds and two ounces. The old fisherman could not believe that Freddy's fish, which was 10 inches shorter than Lunker's, could outweigh Lunker's fish. The old fisherman said "I've been fishing these waters for 50 years and I've never seen anything like this". Nevertheless, the scales didn't lie and Freddy received $140.00 on behalf of his three-man team.

Lunker's team was pissed and asked for a second weighing just to make sure. The results were identical to the first weighing.

Just before he left the dock, Lunker asked the fisherman to cut open Freddy's fish, and the fisherman obliged. Inside the belly of Freddy's fish were a couple of pounds of rusty nuts, bolts, nails, old fishing lures, coins, a screw driver, and other items that fish don't normally eat.

Lunker immediately lodged a protest but the "biggest" fish money had already been paid out.

There were allegations, none of which were ever proven, that members of Freddy's team had spent some time in the engine compartment of the skipper's boat searching for heavy items that could be stuffed down the mouth of a fish.

After a full investigation, it was determined that the winning fish had been a "bottom feeder" and this accounted for his unusual diet. Freddy's team was absolved of all responsibility for the contents found in the fish's belly and his team gladly spent the prize money.

# 49. A SEVEN IRON "SLICE"

The Leavenworth, WA Golf Course is a pretty golf course that is located next to the Icecycle River. The course has lots of trees and a few hills. It is a good test for the weekend golfer.

A couple of foursomes from Spokane decided to motor down to Leavenworth and play a couple of rounds of golf over a long weekend. Leavenworth is about a four-hour drive from Spokane.

After checking in to a motel located nearby, the guys headed for the course. It wasn't long before Bill and Mel made a challenge to Lunker and Knob. The wager would be $5.00 per hole per player.

The first eight holes moved along without incident. Lunker and Knob were ahead by $10.00 each heading to the ninth hole. Bill and Mel pressed on the ninth hole.

Hole number nine is a steep uphill hole to a blind green and the fairway is lined with trees. Knob was the last one to hit and hit his ball into the trees just off the right side of the fairway. His ball was located about half way up the hill and was lying next to some tall willow branches. Being left-handed, Knob could not get a good swing at his ball. Unless of course he had his partner Lunker, hold the willows back while he swung.

Now holding back willow branches for your partner is not exactly legal in the game of golf. But then with this group, not everyone always played by the rules. And if your opponents were already up on the green and out of sight, what harm could it do? Plus, the press was on and a team certainly didn't want to lose a press on a technical issue such as willow branches.

So Lunker grabbed the troublesome willow branches and held them back as Knob took a practice swing. Perfect. There would be no problem swinging that seven iron. As he went into his backswing, Knob extended his swing a little further than on his practice swing. The seven-iron caught Lunker flush on top of his head. Lunker's white golf hat was soon crimson red with blood. The blow had left a four-inch cut and it was bleeding profusely. Knob had some tape in his golf bag and soon taped a napkin to the top of Lunker's head.

When Lunker and Knob got up to the green and explained that Lunker had suffered an unfortunate injury that would cause a cancellation of the remainder of the match while Lunker went for stitches, Bill and Mel said: "Oh no. A bet is a bet. If you quit, you lose $5.00 per hole. Let that be a lesson to you assholes for cheating". They had a point.

After putting out on nine, Lunker went into the clubhouse which also had a small restaurant. The lady running the restaurant saw that Lunker needed medical attention. She took him into the kitchen area, put his head under the sink water faucet, and cleansed the wound. She then found a first aid pad and taped it to Lunker's head.

Then the match continued for the back nine holes. There was no sympathy—absolutely none---from Bill and Mel.

Lunker and Knob ended up winning $30.00 each that day and it brought great satisfaction being that their opponents refused to cancel the match because of injury.

After the match was concluded, Lunker was taken to the Leavenworth Hospital Emergency Room, where after waiting for another hour and a half, he finally got ten stitches in the noggin.

To this day, Lunker thinks the seven iron to the head was an intentional act by his partner. And every once in a while, he points to the scar as a reminder of another great day on the links.

# 50. THE PUTTING GAME

One year, instead of going back to Montana, the group decided to head to British Columbia for three days of golf. They would play Trickle Creek, Grey Wolf, and St. Eugene's Mission, all great courses.

Rollie was one of the 24 guys on the trip. He was the guy with the ugly, bright green golf bag. Rollie had received the bag many years before while playing for the Chicago Black Hawks. He had been named first star of the game and the bag was his reward. Even though the bag was not very pretty, it had "sentimental" value and Rollie wasn't yet ready to part with it.

On this particular day, the guys decided to introduce a little side game, just to make things interesting. Each group would keep track of the putts that each player took on each hole. At the end of the match, each golfer's total putts would be tallied. Each putt had a value of $1.00. Each golfer who had more putts than another golfer, would pay that golfer $1.00 for each putt that his total exceeded the total for that other golfer. For example, If Joe had 30 total putts for the day and Jack had 25 total putts, Joe would pay Jack $5.00. Each golfer would compare his putts with the other 23 golfers and would either pay the others, or would receive money from the others.

The group was playing Trickle Creek this particular day. It is a beautiful course located just a few miles from Kimberley.

Rollie got off to a bad start and things only got worse. By the end of the round, he had more putts than anybody else---by far. So when he sat down in the clubhouse with his foursome and the putts were tallied, he immediately paid the other three guys to satisfy the putting debt.

Rollie thought he had fully paid his putting debts for the day. But the guys from the other four somes said "Not so Quick Rollie". He did not realize that he also had to pay everybody else in the group of

24 who had fewer putts than him. By the time he was done paying everyone, he had paid out well over $200.00.

That was the only time the group played the putting game. And Rollie's "friends" were nice enough to pick up his dinner tab that evening.

# 51. PLAY ME A TUNE

The guys had just finished playing Buffalo Hills in Kalispell. They boarded their bus, all 24 guys, and headed to Moose's Saloon in downtown Kalispel.

This was the group's second trip to Montana and for most of the guys it was their first "Montana Trip" and most had never had the pleasure of visiting Moose's before.

Moose's is a landmark watering hole in Kalispel. It is well known for its cold beer, hot pizzas, and free peanuts by the shell. All peanut shells are thrown on the floor. The floor is covered with sawdust and at the end of each evening, the janitor sweeps the floor, sawdust, peanut shells, and all, to get it ready for the next day's activities.

One other thing that Moose's is famous for is its funny looking horn (trumpet). If a customer is able to blow the horn and make a noise on his first attempt, that customer wins a pitcher of the coldest beer on the planet.

On this trip into Moose's there were several guys lined up to win the free pitcher of beer. At the head of the line was Franseen who had relatives that ranched in the Kalispel area, some of whom were present in the bar. It seemed only proper that Franseen have the first go at the horn.

Franseen bellied up to the bar and said: "I would like a shot at that free pitcher of beer. Bring the horn over".

The bartender went over and picked up the horn and laid it on the bar in front of Franseen. "Here you go cowboy" said the bartender. "Blow when you are ready".

Well, this particular horn was not an ordinary horn. A normal horn is straight and flares out at the end where the sound comes out. On this horn, the flared end is bent up and back so that it is points directly at the person blowing the horn.

A large crowd had gathered to watch Franseen win the pitcher of beer. Franseen was determined to not let them down. The crowd started chanting: "Franseen, Franseen".

He picked up the horn, took a deep breath, and blew as hard as he could. A huge cloud of baking flour blasted out of the end of the horn into Franseen's face, but no sound came from the horn. Franseen started to sputter and cough. The crowd gasped as their man dropped the horn onto the floor. There would be no free pitcher of beer on this night.

The rest of the golfers started to laugh as they looked at their defeated comrade. His face looked like a big snowball; everything but his eyes were covered by flour.

The last anyone saw of Franseen was in the men's room with his head in the sink trying to get the flour out of his ears.

Welcome to Moose's.

# 52. THAT'S DIRTY!

The boys had just finished a nice round of golf at Wandermere Golf Course on Spokane's north side. The foursome decided to stop at the Stir Lounge located on North Division to have a drink and settle up the games. Nacs was a member of the foursome.

The guys were seated for about 30 minutes when a couple of nice looking, and professionally dressed, women came in and sat at the next table. Nacs soon struck up a conversation with the two and learned that they were real estate sales agents for a Spokane Real Estate Company. Nacs introduced himself, told the ladies that he also was in real estate, and exchanged business cards with the two ladies.

Soon thereafter the foursome split for the evening and went their separate ways.

The next day, Nacs was seated in his office when the front receptionist for his company delivered a nice bouquet of flowers to him. The card that accompanied the flowers said: "Dear Nacs: I enjoyed meeting you yesterday at the Stir. Hopefully we can get together soon and have a drink." It was signed "Kaitlin" who was one of the ladies that he had met the day before.

Nacs was pumped.

The next day Nacs called Kaitlin. When she answered Nacs said: "Hi Kaitlin. This is Nacs. We met at the Stir a couple of days ago. I just called to say thank you for the beautiful flowers you had delivered to me. Would you be available later this week to have a drink?"

There was a long pause on the other end of the phone. Finally, Kaitlin said: "What flowers are you talking about? I didn't send any flowers to anyone."

Nacs knew immediately he had been set up. He just wasn't sure who the culprit was.

His investigation is continuing.

# 53. MICHELANGELO AT WORK

No one's quite sure how Shayff's golf shoes ended up in Tim's truck that day. Apparently, Tim and his buddy, Danny J, dropped Shayff off at Shayff's house after golf; Shaff removed his clubs from the bed of Tim's truck but forgot to take his golf spikes. That's the most logical of explanations. But "how" it happened or "why" that oversight happened is really not important.

The really important point here is that Tim and his sidekick, Danny J, have great artistic talents, and when they combine their imaginative skills, some pretty interesting things are sure to happen.

When this duo got back to Danny J's apartment and realized that their buddy, Shayff, had left his nice white golf spikes in the back of Tim's truck, they quickly realized that the shoes needed a little "tune up". So out came the paint and brushes.

First, they started on the left shoe. A nice, bright, pink color would suit their ex-football linebacker friend just perfect. And so, they applied a coat of pink over the entire left shoe. How pretty! They were sure that Shayff would like it.

Then on to the right shoe. No sense in having both shoes the same color. How about a lime green color for the right shoe. And "voila", within a few minutes the right shoe had been transformed into a beautiful lime green color.

Now let's put the two shoes side by side and see how they look. Fantastic! On Shayff's next trip to the course he will be all style.

The problem now was to get the shoes back to Shayff's house, and into his golf bag without him knowing. Not a problem. The duo called Shayff's girlfriend and made arrangements to get inside the garage while Shayff was at work.

A week or so later, Tim and Danny J invited Shayff to Downriver Golf Course for a round of golf. They were present when Shayff unloaded his golf bag from his car and carried his bag to the clubhouse. They were also present when Shayff opened his bag to get his golf shoes and saw his lime and pink shoes for the first time. Shayff held the shoes up and said: "Damn, are those pretty?"

Everyone in the clubhouse had a good laugh that day. Shayff looked splendid in his new footwear. He continued to wear the shoes for the rest of that golf season.

# 54. "PISSED"

The guys had just put in three hard days in Montana. There had been three rounds of golf and two long nights hanging out in Downtown Whitefish. It was Sunday evening and the bus had just left the Talking Bird Saloon in St. Regis where the boys had sat for a couple of hours "spending" the Kangaroo Court fine money. A few of the guys were tired, and rather than get involved in another Stook game, they decided to have a quick nap before they got after the last of the Kokanees.

Terry is just a little guy in terms of height, but he has bulked up a lot since getting married. There is something to be said for that "home cooking".

Terry doesn't get away from the home front very often but when he does, he makes it worth-while. Such was the case on this trip. He may have set a new bus record for Kokanee consumption over these three days.

Anyway, shortly after leaving The Talking Bird Saloon, Terry had downed a couple of Crown Royals over ice. A perfect ending to a great trip. He then inclined his seat back to the maximum degree and soon nodded off. Red saw an opportunity. He took several ice cubes and gently laid them on the lap of Terry's tan shorts.

Thirty miles went by and the ice cubes started to shrink in size. Terry never moved. After another thirty miles the lights of Spokane were coming into view and by this time, the ice cubes had pretty much melted. Terry was still sawing logs. As the bus headed into Spokane and pulled into the Eagles Ice Arena, which was the unloading point for the trip, the interior lights of the bus came on and Terry finally awoke.

The guys started unloading the bus and headed for their respective vehicles. Some of the guy's wives were waiting for their husbands in the parking lot. Terry's wife was one of those who had come to the rink to pick up her husband. Terry picked up his clubs and suitcase from the bus and wobbled towards his wife who was patiently waiting for her little "sweetheart". As he got to the car his wife noticed that Terry had "peed his pants" and immediately lit into him. For the first time Terry looked down and saw that the front of his tan shorts was indeed very wet. Before he could say anything in his defense, a couple of the guys walked by and told his wife that Terry had consumed a little too much alcohol and had an unfortunate accident. They asked her to not be too hard on him, it could happen to anyone.

Terry still didn't know how the front of his shorts got wet. But the evidence was overwhelming. He didn't have any explanation as he got into his wife's vehicle and headed towards home.

Terry's wife never allowed him to go on another Montana Golf Trip.

# 55. NO ONE HOME

I t was 2:00 AM on an early Sunday morning in downtown Whitefish. The bars were just closing. It had been an exceptionally long day and night. The guys were scattered all over town. Some had found a restaurant for an early morning breakfast; some had walked towards the barbeque hot dog stand to grab a "dog" before turning in for the night; and then there was Franseen.

Franseen decided to head straight back to the Downtowner Motel where the group usually stayed when in Whitefish. The Downtowner was a perfect location for the group because it was located only a block from the main drag and within easy walking distance.

When returning to the Downtowner from the main drag of Whitefish, the closest route is to duck down an alley, walk about 100 yards, crank a left turn, and "voila"---there's the Motel. This is the route that Franseen took as he walked back towards the Motel, by himself, following the night's activities. Franseen's roommate, Nellie, was about 50 yards behind Franseen and was following him back to the Downtowner.

As Franseen ducked down the alley, he came upon a door in the side of a building. He thought the building was the Motel, but in fact it was the door to a phone company's offices. The Motel was one building further down the alley. Franseen pulled his Motel keys out and tried them in the door. No luck. He started banging on the door and yelling for his roommate to open up. Still no luck. Franseen was now starting to get really mad and was banging harder and yelling even louder. Nellie was watching, and enjoying, the entire episode from about 25 feet away. When it looked like Franseen was at the height of his aggression, Nellie walked up and said: "Franseen, what's going on?" Franseen said: "They gave me the wrong F------ key for the room." Nellie said: "Why don't we go one building over and try your key there?"

157

The two guys walked about 40 yards further down the alley and there was the Motel. Franseen looked at Nellie and said: "I think I had one too many tonight."

# 56. WELCOME BACK COXIE

Coxie had just relocated back to Spokane after several years of living in Seattle. He had joined the guys for his first round of golf since returning to the area. Wandermere Golf Course had been the venue.

After golf, the group met at Mama Mia's on Spokane's north side to have a beer and a good Italian dinner and to welcome Coxie back to town. It was nice to have him back. Jerry, the owner of Mama's, had some of the best Italian food in the country and always treated the guys right.

During the course of the evening, Coxie excused himself to go to the men's room. He left his wallet and checkbook on the table. Nellie hurriedly grabbed the checkbook, tore out one check, wrote it to "cash" for $600.00, and signed Coxie's name to it. Although the check was for a large amount, Jerry had no problem cashing it because he knew the guys well.

Coxie returned to the table shortly thereafter and the group finished a nice meal and drank some fine wine. Some good conversation took up the rest of the evening until the group was ready to break up for the night.

Just before the group headed out the door, Nellie stood up and said he had a little "something" for Coxie from the boys. He handed Coxie the $600.00 in cash and said he knew Coxie and family had some pretty hefty relocation expenses and "this was the least the guys could do for a dear friend. And we welcome you back to our city."

Coxie was in tears as he accepted the money. In a broken voice, he thanked the guys "for being such a great group" and he would "never forget their generosity". With that said, the group broke for the evening and the guys headed to their respective homes having a warm feeling in their respective hearts.

About a month later Coxie got a statement from his bank. As he tried to balance his bank book, things weren't making sense. He went over it and over it but things just weren't adding up. He kept asking himself "where did I write a check to cash for $600.00?"

Finally, he remembered the $600.00 "relocation gift" that he had received from his friends just a month before. His first reaction was: "There is no way my friends would do such a thing." Then he thought about it some more and said to himself: "Yes those bastards would."

He was right.

# 57. FATHER JUSTICE

The boys had just finished a great day of golf at Meadow Lakes Golf Course located at Columbia Falls, Montana. The crew was staying in Whitefish and the bus had to pass right past The Blue Moon Café and Bar on the way back to Whitefish. A perfect place to stop for a cold beer.

As was customary, there were 24 guys on board that day, not counting the driver. The entire group was warmly welcomed by the wonderful staff of The Blue Moon.

During the course of the stop at the bar, one of the guys known as "Dodger", so named because he had a habit of "dodging" out just before a bill was to be paid, went to the restroom but inadvertently left his wallet sitting on the table. Freddy, seeing a great opportunity to get "the tight little bastard", quickly removed a credit card from the wallet, gave it to the cocktail waitress and told her to take an impression of the card and return it immediately to Freddy. The waitress complied and returned the card to Freddy, who replaced the card in the wallet. The Dodger returned to his table shortly thereafter.

The guys spent 90 minutes or so in The Blue Moon. Several rounds of drinks were purchased and each time Freddy said: "Put it on my card". The Dodger was having a great time, especially because he knew someone else was picking up the tab---again. What a perfect day for The Dodger.

Word spread among all the guys, except for the Dodger, just what was happening with the drink tab. It was also decided that at a certain time all the guys, except for The Dodger, would start leaving the bar and would board the bus, leaving The Dodger as the last one in the bar. The plan worked to perfection. All the guys had left the bar and headed to the bus. The Dodger, being the last one in the bar, finished his drink and realized that the bus was getting ready to leave. He got up and headed towards the door. The cocktail waitress came over to him and said: "Are you mister (last name)?" The Dodger replied: "Yes I am." The waitress said: "I have your credit card tab ready for your signature." She handed the tab to The Dodger so he could verify the name. Sure enough, it was his credit card. The tab was $340.00---without tip.

The Dodger looked around for help but all his "friends" had left to board the bus. He was stuck. He had no alternative but to sign the tab. Whether "the tight little bastard" left a tip is unknown.

The boys had a great laugh when The Dodger boarded the bus. He received many "thank yous" from the guys. But he sulked for the entire rest of the trip. He never made the trip again.

Sometimes "Justice" has an unusual way of working.

# 58. LITTLE GUY WITH A BIG CLUB

I t was unfortunate that the Judge's clubs fell off the cart just as the Judge was pulling on to the paved pathway at Downriver. It was even more unfortunate when the clubs hit the paved surface and snapped off the head of the Judge's driver. It was probably another defective strap on the power golf cart. After all, Downriver had a history of defective straps on their carts.

Nonetheless, and for whatever reason, Knob felt somewhat responsible for the damage done to the driver and, being the gentleman he is, told the Judge that he would get the Judge a new shaft for the driver. "Just give me a few days and I will get your driver back to you" said the generous Knob.

On the following Saturday, the Spokane Old Timers Hockey Association was hosting its annual tournament at Wandermere Golf Course. A full contingent of golfers, 144 total, was signed up for the tourney. The Judge was teamed up with the Doc in one cart and Knob and Lunker were riding together in another cart thus making up the foursome.

A couple of days before the tourney Knob called the Judge and told him his driver would be ready by the Saturday tournament and that Knob would bring it to the course. That was fine with the Judge. "Oh, by the way, Lunker and I will take on you and the Doc on Saturday, even up, $1.00 per hole per person" said Knob. "You are on" said the Judge.

"There is only one condition" said Knob, "You can't practice with your new driver before the match starts, and you have to use your new driver to tee off on every hole but the par threes---none of this 'hitting iron off the tee bullshit". The Judge was so happy to have a driver back in his bag that he said "Agreed".

What a slam dunk this will be, thought the Judge. Doc is an 8 handicap and the Judge is a 22. Lunker is a 15 handicap and Knob is a

28. What's not to like about this matchup? Even with a new driver it's a "no brainer."

Saturday morning arrived and the course was overflowing with golfers ready to tee off in the shotgun start. Knob spotted the Judge on the putting green getting in a little practice before the big match. He walked over to the Judge and handed him his new driver. "What the hell is this?" asked the Judge as he observed his new driver for the first time.

The new driver was not exactly like the old one. The shaft on the new one was exactly nine feet long and for the 5-foot 5-inch Judge, it promised to be somewhat of a "challenge" during the upcoming match. Both the Judge and his partner, the Doc, complained about the club but they realized that they had agreed previously that the Judge would use the club and that was the end of the argument.

On his first tee shot attempt of the day, the Judge missed the ball entirely. He tried to persuade his opponents to grant him a mulligan, but that request fell on deaf ears. His second swing with the monster club resulted in the Judge hitting the ball right off the toe of the club onto the adjoining fairway. And so, it went for 18 holes. The Judge never hit one decent drive the entire day. And with the Doc and the Judge unsuccessfully "doubling up" on the par threes, they ended up losing $34.00 each to Lunker and the Knob. It really hurt when they had to dig out the green backs and pay their worthy opponents.

The Judge and the Doc thought there was a lack of good "sportsmanship" exhibited that day but every other golfer who watched the interesting driving exhibition that the Judge put on, sure got a kick out of the "little fella with the big club."

# 59. THE "MOUSE --TURD" COP

The two foursomes had just completed an afternoon round of golf at Indian Canyon Golf Course in Spokane. The guys had worked up a good thirst in the hot July sun. The sidewalk patio outside of O'Dougherty's Bar & Grill in downtown Spokane, seemed like the perfect place to unwind, square up the golf games, and get some late afternoon shade, something the group had not seen in five hours.

It was about 5:40 PM when the group of eight found a couple of open outside tables right next to the city sidewalk and about 15 feet from Spokane Falls Boulevard. They ordered a couple of pitchers of beer and sat back to relax.

A few minutes after sitting down, the group observed a City Meter Cop pull up in his little covered scooter and stop next to a car that was parked at a City parking meter. It was now about three minutes before 6:00 PM. Come 6:00 PM, there is no longer a requirement that money be placed in a meter.

Out gets the Meter Cop with his ticket book. "I will write one last ticket before I call it a day" the cop must have been thinking.

The Cop walked up onto the sidewalk and started writing a ticket. It was now about one minute before cut off time. And yet there he was, and by golly he was going to write until the bell struck 6:00 PM.

Nellie was one of the eight golfers sitting in the outdoor patio at O'Dougherty's that afternoon. When he saw the dedicated Meter Cop still writing a ticket at one minute to six, Nellie picked up a yellow plastic mustard container and made an overhand lob towards where the cop was standing. The mustard container hit the sidewalk about three feet in front of the cop. The top flew off the container and the mustard contents spewed out covering the cop's nice blue uniform from about the waist down to his black polished shoes.

The cop immediately looked into the patio area to see who had done the dirty deed. There was no obvious guilty party so the cop asked "Who threw the mustard container?" No one answered but by now everyone saw the mustard covered cop and all enjoyed a great afternoon laugh at the expense of one of Spokane's finest.

The cop was last seen putting the ticket on the car's windshield. He wasn't going to let anything, not even a good dosing of mustard, stop him from giving out that last ticket.

# 60. THE COFFEE AND THE CROW

Pumpkin Ridge is a beautiful Golf Course located in Portland, Oregon. Several of the Spokane guys had traveled to Portland to attend a wedding of one of their friends. While in Portland, a group of four decided to play Pumpkin Ridge.

The group teed off at 8:15 am. It was a nice June Saturday. They would have plenty of time to get in their round of golf and still make the 4:00 pm wedding.

Frankie and the Judge rode in one cart while Lunker and the Knob rode in the other.

Being a morning tee time, all four had purchased a coffee to go, in the clubhouse and had taken their Styrofoam cups to their respective carts where they had placed them in the cup holders.

The Judge had started off poorly, which was really not much of a surprise. On the second hole he had knocked his tee shot far into the trees on the right side. He went by foot in search of his ball while the other guys went to play their shots on the fairway.

Just before Lunker hit his second shot, he saw several earthworms on a damp mound not far from his ball. He grabbed one of the worms and placed it into the Judge's coffee cup. Lunker then played his second shot and ultimately played out the hole. The Judge located his ball in the right trees, chipped out, and also played out the hole.

The group played the third hole without incident, with each of the four golfers sipping on their coffees.

When the foursome got to the fourth tee box, the Judge took a draw on his coffee and started to cough. He had discovered a foreign substance in his coffee cup. He spit into his hand and lo and behold there was an earthworm that would cause any fish to salivate.

The Judge threw the worm onto the ground and immediately

started throwing out obscenities.

None of the other group members knew anything about any worm. The closest they could come to solving the riddle was when Frankie spoke up and said he had seen a crow with a worm in its mouth on the prior hole, the inference being that the crow had either dropped the worm into the cup accidently, or placed it in the cup for safe keeping. The Judge, being the wise man that he is, didn't buy either of those possibilities.

# 61. CAR FOR SALE---CHEAP!!

The Priest River Golf Course is a nice little 9-hole, tree lined course located about an hour northeast of Spokane. The course had two sets of tee boxes and in order to play 18 holes, each player would play from one set of tees on the first nine holes, and from the second set of tees on the back nine.

Dash was scheduled to play in a Food Broker's tournament at the Priest River Course and needed to put a foursome together. He asked Nacs and Tim to join him and a co-worker to make up his foursome. They agreed to meet at the Screaming Yak Restaurant and Bar, in north Spokane, the following Saturday at 8:00 am. They would then hop into one car and ride together to the Priest Lake course.

Saturday arrived and the four met as scheduled. After having a quick breakfast at the Yak, the group hopped into Dash's car and headed to the Course.

Nacs left his bright green Chevy Tahoe parked in front of the Yak facing Francis Avenue, which is one of the busiest arterials in the City.

Before leaving for the golf course, Tim went into the Yak's office and talked to his friend, Todd, the owner of the Yak.

The golf match was going along fine. Dash's foursome had just finished the fourth hole when Nac's cell phone rang. The other three guys could here Nacs say: "My car is not for sale; I really think you must have the wrong number."

The group continued playing into the sixth hole when Nac's phone rang again. Once again Nacs could be heard saying: "Yes, it is a bright green color, and yes, it is located in the Yak parking lot, but it is not for sale." The guys asked Nacs if their golf game was interfering with Nacs business transactions. To which Nacs responded that some guy was calling about buying Nacs car and the car wasn't for sale.

The group made the clubhouse turn but not before there were a couple of more inquiries about the good price that Nacs was asking for his car. His Chevy Tahoe was only two years old and, according to the callers, a sign on his car was listing the car for sale for $6000.00 "but it has to be sold today."

Nacs knew there had to be a mistake. But the calls kept coming throughout the rest of the match. In fact, one caller asked Nacs whether he would consider painting the vehicle another color as a condition of sale "Because I don't like the bright green color." With his frustration now starting to show, Nacs replied: "No I won't paint my car because it's not for sale."

The golf finally came to an end but the calls didn't. All the way back to Spokane, his cell phone continued to ring non-stop.

When Dash pulled into the Yak parking lot, there was Nac's car right where he had parked it seven hours earlier. But stretching across the entire front windshield was a sign that said: "Car for sale $6000.00. Must be sold today." In big black numerals was Nacs' cell phone number.

The car probably had a value of close to $20,000.00. Now Nacs understood why there was so much interest in his car. He immediately ripped the sign off his car and went inside the Yak to find out who was responsible for placing the sign on his car. No one saw anybody place the sign. They did however say that there had been several people stop and inspect the vehicle.

Several days later a rumor surfaced that implied that Tim and Todd, the owner of the Yak, had prepared the sign before Dash's crew headed for Priest River and that the sign had been placed by Todd after knowing that Nacs would be in the middle of his round of golf. The rumor was never confirmed.

# 62. JULY 4TH SPARKLERS

Dear Park, Washington is a small bedroom community of 2500 people located about 12 miles north of Spokane. The Deer Park Golf Course is a flat 18-hole course.

Each 4th of July weekend, Deer Park used to have a parade and a three-day rodeo. The rodeo would have performances on Friday and Saturday evenings, and Sunday afternoons. It would also have various carnival-like rides and attractions and an outdoor dance on Saturday night following the rodeo. It was the biggest "happening" of the year for Deer Park and was a fun event.

One year a group of eight guys from Spokane decided to play the Deep Park course on a Saturday afternoon and then attend the rodeo and festivities that evening. Nellie was one of the eight guys.

The group decided to meet at a central location In Spokane and take two cars to Deep Park. However, Nellie opted out of the car-pooling arrangement and decided to drive his own car to Deer Park because he had arranged a date with a "hot chick" he had been pursuing for some time. He was to meet her at nine PM after she got off work. Nellie knew that the rest of the guys would not likely be back in town by date time.

The group played the Deer Park course in uneventful fashion and then headed to the carnival and rodeo grounds to wander around and have a beer before that evening's rodeo performance.

One of the "events" that the guys spent a little time playing, was the "chicken square" contest, which was set up by the local Kiwanis Club to raise money for its charity. The "chicken square" contest consisted of a large board that looked like a large checker board. It was about 10 feet square in size. The board had a total of 100 different colored squares, with each colored square having a different monetary value. The board was located under a large tent, without sides, that provided shelter from the elements. The players would make bets on which colored square a chicken would shit on, and if the player guessed correctly, the player would receive winnings in an amount that was several times what he bet. It was sort of like a roulette game only a chicken would be released and would be allowed to freely roam over the board until he took a dump. It was a fun game to play.

After playing the "chicken square" game for an hour or so, and having a couple of beers, the group walked over to the rodeo grounds to watch that night's performance. The guys tried to convince Nellie to stick around for the rest of the evening and call off his date. But no amount of talk could convince Nellie to by-pass the date that he had worked so hard to get.

About 40 minutes before Nellie was scheduled to leave Deer Park to return to Spokane for his rendezvous, Freddy and Lefty left the rodeo grandstands to get a round of beer for the group. They returned several minutes later with the beer. Not long after, Nellie announced that he was leaving for Spokane and said good night to the rest of the guys. He left the grandstand and headed towards his car which was parked on the main drag next to the rodeo grounds.

As soon as Nellie started walking towards his car, Freddy and Lefty motioned to the rest of the group to come with them and follow Nellie as he made his way to his car. When Nellie got to his car, he found that both rear wheels had been completely removed and were nowhere in sight. The rear wheel hubs were sitting on the pavement. Nellie started to cuss. He had a date in about 30 minutes. He did not want to miss it. He looked around and saw the rest of the group watching and laughing from about 50 feet away.

Nellie got into his car, started it up, and started driving down the road, as sparks started to fly from the rear hubs. Lefty, now becoming concerned that Nellie could do irreparable harm to his car, or that the flying sparks could possibly cause a fire, ran after the car and flagged it down. He convinced Nellie to pull the vehicle over while they replaced the rear wheels. The wheels were replaced, Nellie headed into Spokane, and he made his date on time.

Nellie did not see the humor in the actions of his friends that day. But the story continues to be told and always draws a laugh.

# 63. ITS HEAVIER THAN IT LOOKS

The foursome had met at Wandermere Golf Course on a Friday afternoon for a 1:30 PM tee time. The temperature that July day was in the 90's. Bobby and Herb, the owners of the private course, always gave the guys "special preference" when they made a "late call" and asked if the Course could "squeeze them in". This day was no exception.

Rollie, who was in his mid-60s at the time, arrived about an hour before the scheduled tee time and announced that on this day he was going to walk rather than ride in a cart as was his custom. He wanted "to get some exercise". Of course, he had with him his ugly bright green golf bag; he was never going to get rid of that bag; it was the one he had received many years previous for being the first star of the game while playing for the Chicago Black Hawks.

Rollie laid his bag down just outside the pro shop and announced that he was going to grab a quick sandwich before teeing off. He headed into the snack bar.

While he was eating, one of the guys grabbed his golf bag and walked it around to the other side of the Pro Shop where there was a lot of landscape gravel in the flower beds. All of Rollie's clubs were removed and the bottom eight inches or so of the bag was filled with gravel. The clubs were then placed back in the bag. Although the clubs now sat eight inches higher than before, it was not obvious that the bag had been "altered". The bag now weighed about 15 pounds more than previously.

Everybody but Rollie rode in carts that day even though they were all at least 10 years younger than Rollie. He carried his clubs. It was a hot afternoon and there is very little shade on the front nine at Wandermere. Rollie was puffing pretty good by the time he finished the front nine.

On to the back nine. Although he was offered a ride on the

back nine, Rollie refused saying again that his goal was to get "some exercise" even though the temperature was well into the 90s.

Rollie managed to walk the entire back nine, and carried his bag the entire distance. He was obviously "beat" by the time he made it up the 18th fairway to the clubhouse. The comment that he made when he set his bag down at the clubhouse was "whew, that was tougher than I thought".

After squaring up the games over a couple of beers, Rollie walked to his vehicle to drive his vehicle up to the "club drop off area" where he would pick up his clubs and place them in his car. Lunker, who rode to the course with Rollie, picked up his own clubs and Rollie's clubs and walked towards the area to where Rollie had just pulled his car. As he handed Rollie's bag and clubs to him, Lunker said: "Holy s--- Rollie, your bag is twice as heavy as mine. What in hell do you have in there?" Rollie lifted both bags and realized that although the bags were about the same size, his bag was much heavier than Lunker's. It was then that he started to investigate and found that the bottom of his bag was full of rocks and that he had just carried the entire package for 18 holes in extremely hot temperatures.

Rollie knew that there was no sense in trying to find out who was responsible for the extra weight. He had been around this crew too long. Being more vigilant in the future was his only hope.

That was the last time he decided to carry his clubs.

# 64. WHAT ABOUT US??

I t was early Sunday evening, about 8:00 PM. The 24 guys had just completed three rounds of golf in the Whitefish area. Their bus had stopped at The Talking Bird Saloon and the Kangaroo Court fine money had again been wisely spent. The guys were starting to board the bus for the final leg of the trip back to Spokane.

On the trip for the first time was Coxie Senior, a long-time goaltender from the Canadian province of Manitoba who had come to Spokane 40 years previous to play hockey and never left. Coxie's two adult sons were also on the trip.

Located immediately next to The Talking Bird Saloon at St. Regis, Montana, is a gas and convenience store. Just as the guys were boarding the bus for the return trip to Spokane, Coxie Senior decided to go to the convenience store and purchase three ice cream cones, one for himself and one for each of his two sons. He then walked to the bus, got on, and over the objections of each of his sons, attempted to give a cone to each one of them. The sons refused to take the ice cream from their father realizing that there would be serious financial repercussions if the three family members ate ice cream cones in front of the other 21 guys on board the bus.

It was a hot August evening and Coxie Senior had no problem consuming all three cones himself and, unlike his kids, seemed oblivious to the potential consequences of treating himself in front of the other 21 guys on board the bus.

After Coxie Senior had consumed the last of the three ice creams, and had started to relax in his reclined bus seat, the esteemed Judge of the Kangaroo Court got on the bus microphone and convened a "special session" of the Kangaroo Court to "take up the issue of one of our members consuming three ice cream cones in the presence of the other golfers on board the bus, without thinking enough of his golf mates to also offer an ice cream cone to each of those members".

After learning that the cost for each of the three cones was $3.00, and that there were a total of 24 other people on board the bus, including the bus driver and the two sons of Coxie Senior, the esteemed Judge immediately levied a fine against Coxie Senior in the amount of $72.00.

A most expensive ice cream cone indeed! Justice had again been served and another lesson had been learned.

# 65. A CLEAR VIOLATION OF TRUST

I t was another trip to Montana. Coxie Junior had been in charge of lining up the golf courses that would be played. Now it is important to know that Coxie Junior is about a three handicap and he has his personal "favorite" courses in Montana. He doesn't much listen to the input of the other guys when lining up the courses. Coxie Junior is only interested in playing the courses he prefers.

And so it was on this particular trip. And it just so happened that Coxie Junior won over $300.00 from the KPs, long drive contests, and team games over the three days. He was "gloating" as the boys ate their pizza and drank their cold beers at Moose's Saloon in Kalispel just before boarding their bus for the return trip to Spokane

The other guys on board the bus were pretty upset that one of their own would look after his own needs and not give consideration to the desires of the majority. This is exactly the type of injustice that the Kangaroo Court was meant to correct. And so, as the bus pulled out of Kalispel and started its trip towards The Talking Bird Saloon in St. Regis, the Kangaroo Court was called into "special session" to determine whether Coxie Junior had violated the "trust" that was supposed to exist when he was arranging the golf courses for that three-day trip.

The group as a whole was asked to comment on the situation and voice opinions as to whether Coxie Junior should pay a fine, forfeit all or part of his weekend winnings, or whether some other justice should be levied.

In the spirit of fairness, Coxie Junior was also given the opportunity to present his side of the story and to present arguments that could possibly absolve him from responsibility or at least mitigate his fine.

After due consideration of the 24 voices on board, the esteemed Judge took a vote as to whether Coxie Junior had violated his position of "trust" when scheduling those golf courses that he favored over courses that the majority favored. By a vote of 23 to one, it was determined that Coxie Junior had in fact violated his position of "trust" and appropriate sanctions were in order.

After considering all the evidence, and the "impartial" vote of the other golfers on board the bus, Coxie Junior was required to forfeit all of his $300.00 in winnings, and in addition, pay a fine of $100.00.

With another $400.00 now in the "beer pot", there would be enough money to quench the thirst of the boys once the bus pulled into The Talking Bird Saloon, some 90 miles up the road.

And once again, the Kangaroo Court had carried out its intended function with fairness, precision, and speed.

NOTE: The $400.00 "fine" against Coxie Junior remains the highest fine ever levied against any golfer on the Montana Golf Trip.

# 66. WHERE'S NELLIE?

Nellie was an original and founding member of the annual Montana Golf Trip. For 30 consecutive years the guys traveled to the State of Montana to enjoy three days of golf and companionship. Usually there were 28 golfers on board when the bus left the Eagles Ice Arena in north Spokane on the second Friday of August, at 7:30 am.

About seven years ago, Nellie developed liver cancer and passed away. He was cremated and his ashes were placed in a beautiful wooden urn that was decorated with golf symbols in honor of Nellie. In his last wishes Nellie asked that his ashes be scattered on Mount Spokane, where he had spent hundreds of hours skiing over the years. But before that wish could be carried out, the group decided that Nellie should make one final trip to Montana with the guys.

Nellie's funeral was in May. When the second Friday of August rolled around, Nellie boarded the bus with 28 of his dearest friends and the bus pulled out headed for Montana.

Over the next three days, Nellie took part in all the activities. He rode on the golf carts during the three rounds of golf, he went to the bars with the guys, he had his picture taken with many pretty ladies, and he joined the boys for pizza at Moose's Saloon in Kallispel following the Sunday golf. He was kept busy the entire trip.

On the return trip to Spokane, the bus always stops at the Talking Bird Saloon in St. Regis, Montana. There is usually two or three hundred dollars in "fine money" left in the common kitty, and the guys are determined to stay at the Talking Bird drinking Montana whiskey and vodka until that "fine money" is spent. It usually takes a couple of hours for the boys to drink up that "fine money".

On this particular trip, the guys took Nellie into the Talking Bird Saloon. Nellie visited every nook and cranny in the Saloon and met everyone in the place. He had his picture taken with many of the patrons, and the bar tender said they had never before had a fully loaded urn in the Saloon. To honor Nellie, the bartender set up a free round of Crown Royal shots for the entire bar. Everyone in the Saloon made a toast to Nellie that day.

After a couple of hours of socializing at the Talking Bird, it was time to head for Spokane which was two hours up the road. The guys boarded the bus and headed for home.

About ten miles down the road, Horse yelled: "Who's got Nellie?" Nobody spoke up. Again: "Who's got Nellie?" Again, no response. Now a search of the bus was underway---there was no Nellie.

"Bussy, turn this thing around, we need to find Nellie" demanded Horse.

The bus driver turned the rig around at the first turnoff he could find and the bus headed back to the Talking Bird. Several of the guys went into the Saloon and found Nellie, sitting on a table with three Montana beauties, seemingly having a great time. More photos were taken of Nellie and the ladies and finally, it was time for Nellie to "again" board the bus, this time for real.

It seemed only fitting, that Nellie didn't want his Montana Golf trips to end.

# 67. A COOL DIP ON A HOT DAY

As the bus made its way towards the Polson turn off that would eventually take the 24 golfers to The Talking Bird Saloon in St. Regis, Horse was at the very front of the bus scouting the beautiful coastline of Flathead Lake. It was a hot August afternoon and Horse, along with most everyone on board that day, would give anything for a quick dip in the lake.

Horse alerted Kenny, the bus driver, of his plan to stop the bus if and when a private dock appeared on the left side of the bus. He let the driver know that a lot of the guys wanted a quick dip in the lake.

A few minutes later Horse spotted the private dock he had been searching for. He asked Kenny to pull the bus over at the first turnout he could find. It just so happened that there was a turnout on the right side just ahead. As the bus pulled over Horse yelled to the boys that there was a private dock and swimming area on the left side and that anyone who wanted to take a quick dip should depart the bus.

Fifteen guys got off the bus, crossed the highway, ran down to the private dock in various degrees of undress, and dove into the lake. A middle-aged lady was sitting outside her cabin enjoying the beautiful weather, when all of a sudden there were fifteen guys diving off her dock into the water. As the lady got up and said: "This is private property, you can't do that", the guys were already getting out of the water and heading back to the bus, fully refreshed.

"Thank you Ma'am for your hospitality," said the guys as they ran back to their bus. The lady just stood there not believing what she had just seen.

# 68. "MERRY CHRISTMAS HONEY"

He golfs once a year--- the three rounds on the Montana Golf Trip. Other than that, his clubs are kept under lock and key.

He has made every Montana trip but three; there have been 30 trips.

"Why"? a person might ask. Because he likes beer and he likes a good time.

His name is Charlie.

A few years back, the guys were again on their three-day trip into the great State of Montana. And Charlie had already consumed a 12 pack of Kokanee by the time the bus pulled into the Whitefish Golf and Country Club where the guys would play their first round of golf on the trip.

The Whitefish Course is a beautiful layout cut out of the forest and located not far from Flathead Lake. And the outdoor patio and bar is second to none for the golfer who likes to relax after a day on the course. And it just so happened that there were 24 guys from Spokane who took advantage of that fine outdoor setup following their first round of golf. And a couple of hours later, after consuming fine food and drinks, and enjoying that beautiful Montana fresh air, the guys were ready to head back to the hotel to get cleaned up before taking in the sites and activities of downtown Whitefish.

Charlie had endured a long, tough day on the golf course. He had shot a 124 and although that score was close to his personal best, his golfing partners indicated that "he didn't count them all."

Charlie may have also set a new personal best for Kokanee beer consumed in one 14-hour period. One count was at 33 Kokanees, another was at 41 Kokanees "but that didn't count the ones he drank on the bus" claimed his cart partner, Kicker. An accurate count will not likely be ever known, but one thing for sure is that he drank a lot of beer that day.

In fact, he had consumed so many cold ones that he "fell asleep" on his bed as soon as he got back to his hotel room. And despite several attempts to wake him so that he could accompany the rest of the guys to downtown Whitefish, Charlie wasn't going anywhere. He was out cold.

"What a great opportunity" thought his good friend and roommate, Kicker, who immediately summoned some of the other boys to the room. "Let's get the razor out and shave our good friend Charlie. He will never know who did it and no one will ever tell him."

And so the shaving process started and ended within minutes. Charlie was now completely bald. And he never moved an inch. Pictures were taken—this would make a perfect Christmas card for his EX-wife.

And when one of the guys suggested that they "also shave his head", the response was unanimous "No, that would be a dirty trick to pull on our good friend Charlie"

The "special" Christmas card: "Merry Christmas, Honey. Love Charlie" was timely and thoughtfully sent that Christmas, by someone unknown. Although Charlie's return address was clearly visible on the envelope, he apparently received no reply.

# 69. THANKS FOR THE DONATIONS, DUMMIES

The foursome had just played its first round of golf of the new season, at the Lewiston Golf Course, in Lewiston, Idaho. Lewiston is about 100 miles from Spokane and has a milder climate. The golf courses in Lewiston usually open a month or so before the Spokane courses.

Upon arriving back in Spokane, the guys decided to stop by the Maxwell House Restaurant and Bar for a bite to eat before heading home.

The Maxwell House has been in existence for over 50 years and has been owned and operated by Ricardo and his wife for about 40 of those years. They have been great supporters of Spokane's many hockey teams over the years and Ricardo sometimes makes the Montana Golf trips.

On this particular day Ricardo met the foursome, when they entered the Maxwell House, and showed them to their table. The group soon ordered food and drinks.

The Stanley Cup playoffs were just around the corner and the Maxwell House always has a drawing FOR TEAMS THAT ARE IN THE PLAYOFFS. Each participant throws $20.00 into the pot and draws a team out of a hat. If your team gets to the "final four" you get money. If your team wins the playoffs, you get a good payout.

Nacs and the Judge were part of the foursome who stopped at the Maxwell House that day after golf. Neither one of them follow hockey much. Another member of the group, Franseen, had already entered the drawing and asked Ricardo "whether the drawing had been sold out yet?" Ricardo said there were still two teams left. Nacs and the Judge immediately said they would like to get into the drawing.

Ricardo went back to his office and returned a short time later with a hat. The hat contained two slips of paper, one had the name of "Maple Leafs" and the other had the name of "Senators" printed on the slips. Nacs and Judge each paid $20.00 to Ricardo and each pulled a name from the hat. Ricardo said: "The lottery is now sold out. Good luck gentlemen."

About a month passed and the Judge stopped by the Maxwell House for lunch one day. Ricardo greeted him as always and showed him to his table. During the course of his lunch, the Judge asked Ricardo how his (the Judge's) team was doing in the playoffs "because I haven't been able to find the team's name in the newspaper." Ricardo said "I think they are doing OK."

Another month went by and the Judge again stopped at the Maxwell House for lunch. The Stanley Cup playoffs were over by then but the Judge didn't follow hockey and didn't know that the playoffs were over. Again, the Judge asked Ricardo how his team had done. Ricardo replied: "You didn't win anything." The Judge then asked: "How far did my team get in the playoffs?" Ricardo responded: "Neither your team not Nacs' team even made the playoffs. You guys need to be smarter than that. But thanks for your contribution."

# 70. YOU CAN'T ALWAYS TELL

The 24 guys were about half way through playing Meadow Lakes Golf Course at Columbia Falls, Montana. There is a snack shop building at the turn where the golfers can get a sandwich or hot dog and a cold drink. They then drive up the hill to the 10th tee box.

Right next to the snack shop is a pond containing many cat tails. Tim noticed the swamp and decided to grab one of the cat tails. Each cat tail has a long stem and at the very top it has "a fuzzy thing" that is about the diameter and length of a hot dog.

Tim and his group had stopped at the snack building and ordered refreshments. Tim ordered two hot dogs and quickly ate the weiner from the first one. He then placed the top of the cat tail ("the fuzzy thing") inside the empty bun and covered it with mustard. Just as Tim finished garnishing the first hot dog, Shenny and his group pulled up to the snack building. Tim turned to Shenney, extended the "hot dog" to him and said: "We are lagging behind, here take this, I need to get going." Shenny said: "Well thank you Buddy. Much appreciated." Shenny chomped into the "hot dog, ate the whole thing, and said: "Pretty good but a little on the dry side.

# 71. "I'LL GET IT"

It was Rollie's 65th birthday. They decided to take him to Indian Canyon Golf Course for his birthday to play a round of golf. Dinner and drinks would follow at the Hedge House.

The golf was uneventful and, following the golf, the foursome traveled down to the Hedge House on Monroe Street to see Bones, who was the female proprietor of the establishment and well acquainted with the hockey crowd.

After a few celebratory drinks, a nice dinner, and the customary singing of "Happy Birthday", Geno asked Bones to bring him the bill at the end of the evening. He was going to pick up the tab for Rollie's birthday. Knob also asked Bones to "bring me the bill. I am going to take care of it."

The evening continued on for another hour or so. Knob then said good bye and left the establishment knowing that Geno was taking care of the bill. Shortly thereafter, Geno also left the bar knowing that the bill had been paid by Knob. In actuality neither one of them had paid the bill.

Rollie stayed and had a birthday drink with a couple of other friends. When he got up to leave, Bones brought him the bill. It exceeded $200.00 without a tip. Rollie looked at the bill and said: "Those sons of bitches. They said they were treating me tonight. Even on my 65th birthday they stick me with the bill."

"Just can't rely on your friends anymore," laughed Bones as she took Rollie's credit card to pay the bill.

A few days later Rollie ran into Geno and Knob at another function. "I want to thank you two bastards for sticking me with the tab the other night. The bill was over $200.00. What a nice birthday present."

Geno and Knob looked at each other and each said to the other: "You said you were getting it".

191

A good laugh was had by all and eventually the two reimbursed Rollie for the bill, including tip.

When the three would meet up at future events, Geno or Knob would always say to Rollie: "I will get this Rollie." Rollie would just shake his head and laugh.

# 72. A GUY NEEDS HIS SLEEP

One Friday afternoon after golfing at Ezmeralda Golf Course in Spokane, a group of 12 golfers decided to head over to Weisse's Tavern located in the Central part of Spokane. It was a neighborhood pub operated by the Weisse family. It was a good facility with great food and drinks and an outside patio where the customers could enjoy the fresh air if they were so inclined.

Because it was Friday and none of the guys worked the next day, the guys stayed a little longer than usual. There was live music playing, the place was crowded with revelers, and everybody was having a good time.

Before the guys realized it, midnight was upon them and they decided it would probably be a good time to head towards their respective homes.

Sudsie was one of the twelve guys present at Weisse's that evening and probably had a little more to drink than he should have. Sudsie lived on the South Hill of Spokane which was quite a distance from Weisse's. Being the responsible person that he is, Sudsie decided to have a cup of coffee before heading home. After finishing his coffee, Sudsie felt a little tired and decided to lay down inside his car for a short nap. His car was parked in Weisse's parking lot. It soon became apparent to Sudsie that he could not get comfortable in the back seat of his car. Therefore, he got out of his car and remembered a grassy boulevard located just a couple of blocks west of Weisse's on Ruby Street, which is a very busy north-south arterial in Spokane. What a perfect place for a little nap, especially with the weather being so nice.

Off to the Ruby Street boulevard stumbled Sudsie. When he got to his destination, he was indeed proud of himself for having thought about such an oasis. He laid down on the grass---"wow that felt good. I will just lie here for a few minutes and then head towards home," thought Sudsie as he got himself comfortable.

To this day Sudsie isn't sure whether it was the chirping of the robins or the police officer's voice that woke him from his deep sleep. Whatever it was, it woke him in a hurry. And he could see that the sun was just popping up over the eastern hills. It would be daylight in just a few minutes.

"Could I see some ID please?" asked the officer. "Absolutely" said Sudsie as he embarrassingly fumbled for his wallet and produced his driver's license as the blue lights on the officer's car continued to flash. "What brings you to this neck of the woods on an early Saturday morning?" asked the officer as he gave Sudsie the once over. "I got tied up with some friends and probably had a little too much to drink so I decided to lay down here and have a little nap" responded Sudsie honestly. "I must have missed my ride home" he added.

The sympathetic cop said: "I've probably done a lot worse. I see you live on the South side. Can I order you a cab?"

"That would be great" responded Sudsie, thinking he had just dodged a bullet.

The cab arrived a little while later and took Sudsie home. His wife was waiting for him at the door and wanted answers.

Despite the passage of several years, Sudsie is still reminded of the incident. And the boys are not shy about bringing it up in the presence of Sudsie's lovely wife just to watch Sudsie squirm a little.

# 73. "CRAWLY ANIMALS"

The boys were staying at Francois's luxurious Motel in Tempe. The Motel was the one that included the cockroaches "at no extra charge".

It was Phelpsy's first golf trip to Arizona with the guys. He had heard stories about the Arizona trip but he wanted to experience it first-hand.

There is one little hang up that Phelpsy has that can sometimes be a problem for him, especially in a State like Arizona, where rattle snakes and other varmints are as abundant as orange trees. Phelpsy hates any animal that crawls and he especially hates snakes.

The guys intentionally did not tell Phelpsy about the Motel and its inhabitants. If they had told him that cockroaches were the norm at the Motel, he would not have gone on the trip.

When the three carloads of guys pulled into the parking lot at the Motel, Phelpsy seemed a little reluctant to unload his bags. This was not the type of living quarters he preferred. He usually stayed in a Marriott, Sheraton, Hilton, or some other fancy joint. He was what the boys called "a fancy f___". This Motel did not appear to be up to his standards.

When the other 11 guys started packing their bags into the ground floor units, Phelpsy really had no choice but to go with the flow. His roommate was Lefty, a business partner and certainly a guy he could trust.

At the golf course on the first day of the trip, several of the guys started telling stories in Phelpsy's presence about the many cockroaches that they already had seen in their rooms and they had not slept there yet. Phelpsy was getting edgy. And the banter continued throughout the day. Phelpsy didn't like what he was hearing.

When Phelpsy and Lefty headed back to the motel to shower up before hitting the town, Phelpsy asked Lefty "Do the rooms really have cockroaches in them?" Lefty responded by saying: "The only times you really see them is when it is dark and you turn the lights on. You will see them scatter to all corners of the room. Sometimes they will crawl into your shoes or into anything else that is sitting on the floor. But they really are harmless. They seldom bite unless they get agitated. Only two or three of the guys got bit last time we stayed here."

With those words of comfort, Phelpsy made his way into the shower.

Just walking distance from the Motel is a large store that is part drug store and part department store. It is sort of like a Wal Mart but not quite as big. A person can buy almost anything in that store--- including rubber snakes and other toy crawly animals of almost any size and color imaginable.

Several of the guys quickly made purchases in the "crawley animal" department of that store.

It was after midnight when the guys headed back to the Motel. Lefty, who was Phelpsy's roommate, was pulled aside and asked to delay their arrival back at the Motel for about 10 minutes while the guys, with the help of Lefty's room key, got Phelpsy's room properly set up.

Finally, Phelpsy and Lefty got back to their Motel room. Phelpsy immediately took his shaving kit into the bathroom so he could brush his teeth. When he unzipped the top of the kit, he let out a scream, dropped the shaving kit on the floor, and rushed out of the bathroom. A large black spider was laying on top of his toothbrush. Lefty rushed in, grabbed the spider, and flushed him down the toilet. "You should be okay now" comforted Lefty.

The lights were eventually turned out and Lefty and Phelpsy laid down in hopes of having a good night's sleep.

A few minutes went by and all of a sudden Phelpsy jumped out of bed, turned on the lights, pulled back the covers, and there, laying in between his sheets, was a black, 3-foot-long snake. At first Phelpsy thought it was a real live snake until Lefty grabbed the snake and Phelpsy then realized that it was rubber. Phelpsy said: "That is not funny." Lefty agreed saying: "We will find out tomorrow how it got there."

Phelpsy got very little sleep for the rest of the night.

The next morning Phelpsy went into the bathroom to have a shower and lo and behold there was a real live cockroach sitting in the corner of the shower stall. Phelpsy thought it was a phony until it moved. That was the final straw for Phelpsy. He refused to get in the shower. Instead, he grabbed his suitcase, jammed his clothes into it and said to Lefty: "I am out of here."

After a few minutes of standing in the parking lot, Phelpsy calmed down a little and jumped into one of the cars when it headed to the golf course.

When the crew arrived at the golf course, Lefty was asked to give a blow by blow of the previous night's events. The guys got a great laugh from the misfortunes of their good pal Phelpsy. However, when they came to realize how terrified Phelpsy really was of "crawling things" they decided it would be best if they refrained from any further tormenting of their buddy.

# 74. THE SNORING JUDGE

The guys had been golfing in San Diego for four days one February. The Judge was along on the trip. On the return flight to Spokane, the guys had a layover in Seattle. When they landed in Seattle, the guys located their departure gate. Being that they had 90 minutes to kill before boarding, the guys decided to find a restaurant and get a quick sandwich. The Judge decided to stay at the gate area and read his newspaper. When the guys returned to the gate area 30 minutes later, they found the Judge stretched out across three seats, sound asleep. And he was snoring. Really snoring. When the Judge snores, people in the next county can hear him.

There was still another hour to go before boarding the plane and because of that fact, there weren't any other people at the gate area. So, the guys decided to not wake up the Judge but let him snore to his heart's content.

The guys left the gate area again and wandered around the many shops that were located nearby. When they returned to the gate area 40 minutes later, the ticket check-in clerks were at their usual spots and many passengers were now in the boarding area. And of course, the Judge was still stretched out across three seats and his snores were just a-rumbling throughout the entire area. People were staring at the Judge wondering what was going on. Some were laughing and some appeared upset that he was taking up three seats in a busy gate area.

The Judge's golfing buddies just stood back and laughed wishing that they had a video camera to record the entire thing.

Only when the ticket clerk made an announcement did the Judge finally wake up and look around wondering where he was.

# 75. THE SNORING JUDGE---I NEED OUT

This one happened many years ago before the guys really understood how bad the Judge's snoring really was.

The guys had just finished playing a round of golf at the Chelan Golf Course in Chelan, WA. They had rooms reserved at a local motel. They would stay the night, play another round in the morning, and then head back to Spokane that afternoon.

After the first day of golf the boys checked into the motel, two guys to a room. They then went out for dinner and a few beers and returned to the motel for the night. The Judge and Nellie were roommates.

It wasn't long after turning out the lights that the Judge started snoring---really loud. The Judge only knows one way to snore and that is really, really, loud. No matter what Nellie did he couldn't turn it down. Finally, Nellie got out of bed, packed his suitcase, and headed out the door. It was 2:30 in the morning. He went to the motel office to get another room but all other rooms were occupied for the night. He then went back to his car and drove around Chelan until he found another motel that had a vacancy. He settled in for the night and finally got a decent sleep.

The next morning, Nellie drove back to the motel where the rest of the guys were staying. The first guy that Nellie saw was the Judge, standing outside the motel. The Judge asked: "Where did you get to? I was going to buy you breakfast this morning". Nellie looked at the Judge, shook his head and said "You owe me a night's lodging you little prick".

The Judge never reimbursed Nellie for the cost of the second Motel room.

No one ever roomed with the Judge again, except Rookies who had not yet heard of the Judge's snoring reputation.

# 76. SLEEPING IN THE HALL

This also happened many years ago, before the Judge's snoring notoriety had been well documented.

It was a golf trip to Vancouver. The guys were staying in a nice hotel, 2 guys to a room. Lunker had drawn the Judge as his roommate on this trip.

Shortly after hitting the rack on the first evening, the Judge started snoring. Lunker hit the Judge in the face with his pillow, woke up the Judge, and told him to stop snoring. Back to sleep went the Judge but within minutes he was snoring again. Lunker was going nuts. He knew that he was in for a long night and there was nothing he could do to quiet the Judge.

Lunker had two options: stay in the room and endure the Judge's terrible snoring for the rest of the night and get no sleep; or leave the room. Lunker decided to leave the room. He pulled the mattress off his bed, pulled it out into the hallway and down the hall so it wasn't anywhere close to the Judge's door, and slept there for the rest of the night.

Although he didn't get a great night's sleep, it was an improvement.

## Lesson to be Learned

It is conceded that many people snore. But nobody snores like the Judge. When he is at his best, and that is pretty much every night, the pictures on the wall are rattling and the people in the next room can hear the snoring through the walls. The Judge's snores are long and drawn-out affairs. His whole body shakes and contorts. He has it down to a science. If snoring was an Olympic event, the Judge would win gold every year.

After the above incidents, the word was out. No one would ever room with the Judge again---unless it was a Rookie's first trip.

To this day, the Judge always rooms by himself and pays the extra cost for not having a roommate. This extra expense has cost him thousands over the years but the Judge refuses to see a "sleep specialist/doctor" and refuses to try any of those "snoring gadgets" that are advertised on TV.

It seems that the Judge is forever destined to be the "Lone Ranger" whenever he makes a trip with his golfing buddies in the future.

# 77. JUST TURN THE CRANK, BABY

Some of the guys were playing in Weisse's annual golf tournament at Ezmeralda Golf Course in Spokane. It was a scramble tourney organized by the Judge. The Judge also set the teams in an effort to give all teams a chance at prizes. Many of the golfers had never played before.

Pates had a young lady on his team who had never had a golf club in her hand prior to the tournament. Part way through the first nine she pointed to a rotary ball wash and asked Pates what that was for. He replied: "It is to clean your golf ball. You put your ball in there when it is dirty, then turn that crank to the right so the ball goes past the opening exactly 4 times; then you turn the crank in the opposite direction so the ball goes past the opening 3 times. You then remove the ball, dry it with the towel, and you are ready to hit the tee shot."

For the rest of the round, that lady followed that exact procedure to the amusement of her partners.

# 78. A HISTORY LESSON FROM DAD

The Judge looks a little like Ben Franklin, with the top of his head being bald and long hair hanging down the sides and back of his head. Some of the guys call him "Ben". Ben Franklin's picture or likeness is on every US $100.00 bill.

A few years back, Shayff's son, Max, was seven years old. Shayff brought him to the golf course one day to ride around on the cart while his dad played golf. It just so happened that the Judge was also at the course that day. Shayff gave his son a $100.00 bill and told him: "That's Ben Franklin, our former President. His picture is on this bill. Why don't you go over and ask him to sign it for you."

Max went over to the Judge and said: "Mr. Franklin would you please sign your picture on this bill." The Judge laughingly obliged, and according to Max who is now 18 years old, he still has that now famous $100.00 bill with Ben Franklin's signature.

# 79. DON'T BE RUDE

I t was a late Sunday afternoon at Moose's Saloon in Kalispel. The crew had stopped at Moose's to have their traditional pizza and beer fest before starting their trip back to Spokane. On this particular day, there was a very obnoxious and rude bar tender working the main bar area. He made the guys feel like he was doing them a favor each time he poured one of them a pitcher of beer.

Tim was seated at a table about 20 feet away from where the bartender was working. For some reason, Tim just happened to have with him a blow dart type tube, that was about three times larger in diameter than a regular soda straw. When he heard the guys complaining about what an asshole the bartender was, he wadded up a piece of paper, wet it down good with a mouthful of beer, and blew it through the tube towards the bartender. It struck the bartender right between the eyes and stuck to his forehead. It stung the bartender pretty good. He really wasn't sure what had happened. He looked around in an effort to see who was responsible, but there were no clues anywhere.

# 80. "CARLOS IS A 10"

I t was the annual 4th of July golf tournament at Wandermere Golf Course in Spokane. There were 100 golfers in the scramble tourney including several women. It was a fun tourney although there were some decent prizes given out. The organizer made up the teams with the goal of making the teams as even as possible in an effort to give everyone a chance to win a prize.

Ernie and Charlie, who were both Pit Bosses at Harrah's Casino in Reno, came to Spokane to play in the tourney. Carlos from Spokane also played in the tourney that day. He got partnered up with Charlie. Carlos had only played golf twice in his life prior to this tournament.

Charlie was a good golfer and a serious golfer. He didn't much care for "playing for fun". And it was no different at the July 4th tourney.

As soon as Charlie saw that Carlos was on his team, he started asking questions about what quality of golfer Carlos was. He got the same answer from three different guys: "He is a nice golfer, probably about a 10 handicap. He will be a nice addition to your foursome."

The first hole at Wandermere has a lake located to the right of right-handed golfers teeing off. Carlos, a right hander, teed up his ball, swung and totally missed the ball. He addressed his ball a second time, swung, and knocked the ball right off the toe of his club and into the lake.

Everybody but Charlie was laughing. And Charlie knew he was in for a long day with his "10 handicap" partner.

# 81. A SANDY PAR

The guys were playing the TPC Golf Course in Scottsdale. There are several sand traps on the course. The Doughber was playing in one of the foursomes. On one of the holes on the back nine, Doughber hit his ball into a trap next to the green. It was a deep trap. The guys standing on the green could only see the top of Doughber's head.

Doughber swung at the ball but the ball never made it out of the trap. He swung a second time with the same result. His third, fourth, and fifth swings also failed him as the guys on the green laughed louder and louder. Finally, his playing partners saw an arm come up from the trap and then a ball coming towards the pin and heard a voice yelling: "Incoming."

The Doughber had finally exited the trap. When asked what he had scored on the hole he said: "Par." And the boys laughed some more.

# 82. NO MORE CHIRPING

Rolph, Lunker, and Knob had traveled over to Stoneridge Golf Course just across the Idaho line to play a quick round of golf. Lunker drove the guys over to Idaho in his two-door, half ton pick-up truck. Rolph won all the money that day and, on the return trip, was chirping like a two-tongued rooster.

Rolph was riding in the back seat of Lunker's pickup. Knob was in the front passenger seat. As Lunker drove through downtown Deer Park on the way back to Spokane, he looked over at Knob and winked. Lunker and Knob had been friends for many years and had been through a lot of "wars" together. When Knob saw Lunker's wink, he knew something was "going down"---he just didn't know exactly what, or exactly when. But he knew he had to be on his toes and take the cues from Lunker when "stuff started to happen."

As the pickup made its way through Deer Park, Lunker pulled into a car wash. The car wash had the portable wash wand hanging on the side of the wall and a coin operated mechanism right next to it. Knob knew immediately what Lunker had in mind. Knob got out of the truck and slipped 50 cents into the coin slot to activate the wand. He then grabbed the washing wand, put it through the open passenger window and gave the "two-tongued rooster" a good cleaning.

That put an end to the chirping for the rest of the trip to Spokane.

# 83. WE GOT OUR LIMIT

The boys were on one of their annual Montana Golf trips. Carlos had decided to go along for the first time. However, because he rarely golfed, Carlos decided to drive his own truck because he wanted to do some fishing during the days when the rest of the group were golfing.

On the way over to Kalispel, the bus, as usual, stopped at the Talking Bird Saloon in St. Regis for a couple of hours while the guys had a few beers. The guys then re-boarded the bus and headed towards Kalispel. It was about 7:30 PM. Mac decided to ride with Carlos and follow the bus into Kalispel. This would give Carlos a little company during the trip into Kalispel.

About 15 miles out of St. Regis, Carlos' truck hit and killed a deer. Carlos pulled off to the side of the road and he and Mac pulled the deer off the road and placed it in the ditch. The deer had done quite a bit of damage to the right front of Carlos' truck but the truck was still drivable.

Off they went again towards Kalispel. About 30 minutes later Carlos' truck hit and killed a second deer. Again, Carlos pulled his truck off to the side of the road and he and Mac pulled the second deer off the highway and placed it in the ditch. This time the collision with the deer caused significant damage to the left front of Carlos' truck but it was still drivable.

The bus had been at the Hotel in Kalispel for a good 30 minutes by the time Carlos and Mac arrived. Carlos' truck looked like it had been through a war.

When Carlos got back to Spokane, he took his truck into a body repair shop for a damage estimate. The damages exceeded $6000.00.

What a great introduction to the Montana Golf Trip.

# 84. BOO HOO

It was 8:30 on Saturday morning. The guys were boarding the bus outside the "Downtowner Motel" in Whitefish. They were heading for Big Mountain Golf Course located just outside Kalispel, about 15 miles up the road. The guys had been told several times that the bus would depart the Motel at 8:30 AM, with or without them.

A head count was taken. There were 22 guys on board. Two were missing. They undoubtedly had a late night. "Let's head er on out" came Freddie's voice from the back of the bus. The bus didn't wait for anyone.

The bus arrived at the Big Mountain course and the guys unloaded their clubs, checked in at the Pro Shop, and headed to the range to loosen up before the first tee time.

Just as the first group was being summoned to the tee box, a taxi pulled up. Out jumped Todd and Sean. And they were bitching: "You assholes could have knocked on our door and told us you were leaving. It cost us $60.00 for the taxi."

There was little sympathy to be found from the rest of the guys.

# 85. HEAD COUNT

The Coxie brothers are regulars on the Montana trip. The older brother is called "Big Cox", whether he warrants it or not, and the younger brother is called "Little Cox", whether he deserves it or not. No confirmatory measurements have ever been taken.

There is a standing joke among the guys. Whenever the group is boarding the bus, the guys take a head count. And if the head count is, for example, 22 guys, someone will always say: "Is that with or without Cox"?

Even after hearing it a hundred times, it is still funny.

# 86. JUST NOT HUNGRY TONIGHT

The guys had bussed to the Kelowna, BC, area one summer to play three or four rounds of golf. After the second day of golfing, the guys had located a good bar and restaurant not too far from the hotel. They made their way down to the restaurant and found a table for ten. Max was one of those ten guys.

After having a few drinks, the guys ordered food. Max had been drinking pretty heavily that day and was having a little trouble talking. The waiter brought the meals for the 10 guys and they all started eating. Max took one bite from his plate and his head just dropped straight down with his face falling flush into his plate of food. He was out cold. He stayed that way until the guys were done eating their meal. The guys then took several pictures of Max. Max was then lifted out of his chair, his face was wiped down, and he was transported back to his room.

The photos that were taken were sent to Max's wife just to verify that Max really had been on a golf trip with his pals.

What a thoughtful bunch.

It was the last time Max was on a Montana Golf Trip.

# 87. SNAKE IN THE GRASS

everal years ago, Geno and his buddy were playing a round of golf at a little nine-hole golf course in Idaho. The golf course had sand greens and there was a rotary ball wash at each tee box. To clean his ball, a player would place it in the ball wash, turn the crank a couple of times, the ball would make a revolution or two inside the ball wash, and would then pop out. The player would then dry his ball and tee it up on the adjoining tee box.

Geno and his buddy had just finished playing the third hole. Immediately behind them and approaching the third sand green, were two young ladies in their early twenties. As Geno and his playing partner made their way towards the ball wash, at the fourth tee box, Geno spotted a small garden snake slithering through the grass. He immediately grabbed the snake, placed it into the ball wash and cranked the handle just enough to make the snake disappear inside the ball wash.

Geno and playing partner then teed off and made their way down the next fairway. As they approached their second shots, they could see that the two young ladies behind them had just finished putting out on the third green and were approaching the ball wash. Geno and his playing partner watched as one of the ladies placed her ball in the ball wash and turned the handle. Instead of her ball popping up, out popped the garden snake. The young lady let out a blood curdling shriek that could be heard all across the golf course.

Geno and partner played on. The long-term effect on the two young ladies is not known.

# 88. WHEN AN ACE IS NOT AN ACE

A few years ago, our crew was playing golf at the Nelson, British Columbia, Golf and Country Club. One of our foursomes was playing behind a local group which was waiting to tee off on the 8th hole, which is a par three hole. Play was slow and our foursome was waiting in line for its turn to tee off.

The golf course is very scenic and is located in the mountains overlooking Kootenay Lake. The eighth hole is about 200 yards long and has an elevated tee box.

One of the golfers in the local group hit his tee shot out of bounds into a heavily treed private field. He then placed another ball on the tee and knocked into the cup for a three.

In the clubhouse after the match, our group tried to get the local golfer to buy us a round of drinks, as is the custom for a hole in one. We told him that we were giving him credit for a hole in one despite his unfortunate first tee shot. The golfer said he greatly appreciated our thoughtfulness but he couldn't accept because it would be contrary to "golf etiquette". The local golfer saved at least $100 because of his "golf etiquette". The guys went thirsty that day.

# 89. POPPING OFF HAS A PRICE

Louis had been long time resident of the Spokane area and had been involved in the hockey scene for many years. He was also an avid golfer and was well known to the Montana Golf group. However, he had never been on a Montana Golf Trip before. One year he decided to go along on that summer excursion into Montana.

Louis was a better than average golfer and immediately bought into the various individual and team golf games that the group would organize as the bus pulled away from Spokane headed towards Whitefish and Kalispel, Montana. Louis was drafted onto one of the golf teams for which he would play over the next three golfing days.

At the end of each golf day, the winning team members would receive their payouts and individual payouts would also be made. It just so happened that at the end of day one, Louis' team received the largest payout of any team in the group and Louis received the largest individual payout.

On Day two, Louis again received a nice individual payout and started to chirp a little. And when Louis again received the largest payout on day three, his chirping got even louder. The other guys on the bus were getting restless.

Over three days of golf, Louis, the "newcomer" to the Montana Golf Trip, had won $260.00. After receiving his winnings, Louis was heard to say:

"Thanks for paying for my trip guys".

"What are you guys doing next weekend"?

"Playing golf with you guys is a lot easier than working".

The one-member Judicial Committee decided that the "newcomer" needed to be reigned in.

As the bus left Kalispel on the return trip to Spokane, with its usual stop off at the Singing Bird Saloon in St. Regis, Mt, the Judicial Committee grabbed the mike and asked for the golfers' attention:

Judicial Committee: "Gentlemen, we have a problem. We have a "newcomer" on board this bus who just won $260.00 over the past three days. That can happen on occasion and we congratulate him for his great showing. However, the newcomer has not yet learned the art of winning---to be gracious and thankful for the opportunities presented. Our group was founded on those principles. We must stop this attitude from spreading within this fine organization. Do any of you have any ideas on how to deal with this newcomer? Also keep in mind that no "rookie" has ever before been the big money winner on this trip. Are we going to allow such a terrible precedent to be established this year?"

From the bus passengers in unison: "Fine him. Take his winnings and put the winnings in the beer pot. We need to stop this right now". It seemed like all the passengers were of the same opinion, almost like they had seen similar situations before.

Judicial Committee: "The group has spoken and I must heed their well-reasoned opinion. I hereby fine you, Louis, the sum of $300, payable immediately, to the beer fund."

Upon which Louis, grumbling all the way, walked to the front of the bus and paid his $300 fine, which amounted to $40 more than he had won during the three days of golf.

The beer fund, which had been close to depletion, was now again fully stocked as the bus traveled the last few miles towards the watering hole at the Singing Bird Saloon, St. Regis, Mt.

There was no more chirping from Louis. There would be no "horrible precedent" set this year, not with this crew. And Louis would continue to go on future bus trips and was always "gracious and thankful for the opportunity".

All but one of the bus passengers knew that justice had again been served.

# 90. YOU CAN'T BLAME THE CHEF!

The guys had just completed their third round of golf at Kokanee Springs, just 20 miles up the road from Nelson, British Columbia, and across Kootenay Lake. It was a Sunday afternoon and the boys were homeward bound back to Spokane, WA.

They learned that the Nelson Maple Leafs Hockey Club was hosting a BBQ dinner and fundraiser on an acreage just outside of Nelson, and right on the way home for the golf group. The group decided to stop by and support the Nelson hockey team. When they arrived, they joined about 200 Nelson hockey fans who were already at the event.

After paying for a BBQ steak, the boys went through the line at the outdoor BBQ and placed their respective orders as to how they wanted their steaks cooked. Once each steak was cooked, the person would take his steak to a chair and table set up under a large open-air tent and would eat his meal at one of the tables set up for the hockey fans. Freddy was one of the first to receive his cooked steak. He grabbed a vacant table under the tent and began eating. He had finished his steak by the time some of the others joined him.

The acreage where the fund raiser was being held was owned by a local dairy farmer who had donated the use of his acreage for the event. Some of his dairy cows roamed freely not far from where the BBQ cook out was set up.

After Freddy finished eating, others joined him at his table. Some of the guys remarked that there were some cow paddies laying on the ground near their table. Freddy seized upon that information and grabbed one of those paddies with his fork and placed it on his now empty plate. He then covered the paddy with ketchup. Just as Freddy finished covering the paddy with ketchup, one of the late arriving golfers approached the table, saw the "steak" on Freddie's plate covered with ketchup, and said "how is the steak"? Freddie replied: "The steak is excellent, go ahead and sample it if you don't mind a little ketchup". The friend said: "I think I will". The friend reached down, cut off a hunk of the "steak", and began chewing on it. He soon realized that it was the worst "steak" he had ever tasted. He spit it on the ground and begged for a beer.

The rest of the guys at the table laughed so hard they couldn't eat their own steaks. But they had three hours of driving time ahead of them to talk about the "best steak dinner they ever had".

# EPILOGUE

For the readers' information, the "Montana Golf Trip" is still going strong, although there was a brief interruption due to COVID. Each year there are new recruits on board the bus as it pulls away from the Eagles Ice Arena on the second Friday of August, headed out for three days of golf and entertainment, not knowing what might be in store for them. New and very creative events are being generated each and every year from the imaginative minds of this new generation of "golfers", with each year's group trying to outdo the stories from prior years. It is hoped that such additional stories will one day be reduced to print for the enjoyment of future readers.

To you, the reader, we thank you for sharing this journey with us, and hope you have enjoyed reading these stories as much as we have enjoyed creating them.

# ABOUT THE AUTHOR

Gail K. Holden received his BA degree in economics from Notre Dame University in Nelson, British Columbia, Canada (1968), via hockey scholarship, while playing for the Nelson Maple Leafs hockey club of the WIHL. He received his JD degree, cum laude, from Gonzaga University, Spokane, Washington, (1972), while playing for the Spokane Jets/Spokane Flyers hockey clubs which won the Allan Cup in 1970, 1972, and 1976. He is presently, and has been, a member of the Washington State Bar Association since 1972. He is president and one of the founders of the Nels Venerus Hockey Scholarship Foundation, a 501 (c)(3) non-profit organization, under the Internal Revenue Code, that raises money and provides financial help to Spokane, WA area youth who desire to play hockey but are lacking the financial means to do so.

Mr. Holden was one of the originators of the "Montana Golf Trip" and has been "on board" the Montana bound bus for the great majority of its thirty plus trips. He, together with most of the characters in these stories, resides in Spokane, WA.

Many of the book's characters continue to board the "Montana Golf Trip" bus on the second Friday of August of each year, headed for the great State of Montana, or some other northwest locations, in search of new adventures and stories that will some day chronicle a second edition of "Crazy Tales From the World of Golf".

Printed in Great Britain
by Amazon

29666305R00141